Hayward Gallery
on the South Bank London

Objects *of* *Desire*
The modern still life

9 October 1997 - 4 January 1998
Artists include **Picasso, Matisse, Duchamp, Mondrian, Klee, Dalí** and **Warhol**

Open 10am - 6pm daily. Late nights Tuesday and Wednesday until 8pm
Advance booking and information 0171 960 4242

The exhibition is organised under the auspices of The International Council
of The Museum of Modern Art, New York

Objects of Desire: The Modern Still Life is sponsored by BMW (GB) Limited
in association with The Times

sbc

Meret Oppenheim *Object*, 1936. The Museum of Modern Art, New York. © DACS 1997

GRANTA 59, AUTUMN 1997

EDITOR Ian Jack
DEPUTY EDITOR Robert Winder
MANAGING EDITOR Karen Whitfield
CONTRIBUTING EDITOR, FRANCE Will Hobson
EDITORIAL ASSISTANT Sophie Harrison

CONTRIBUTING EDITORS Neil Belton, Pete de Bolla, Frances Coady,
Ursula Doyle, Liz Jobey, Blake Morrison, Andrew O'Hagan

Granta, 2–3 Hanover Yard, Noel Road, London N1 8BE
TEL (0171) 704 9776, FAX (0171) 704 0474
SUBSCRIPTIONS (0171) 704 0470

FINANCE Geoffrey Gordon
ASSOCIATE PUBLISHER Sally Lewis
SALES David Hooper
PUBLICITY Gail Lynch, Rebecca Linsley
SUBSCRIPTIONS John Kirkby, Mark Williams
PUBLISHING ASSISTANT Jack Arthurs
TO ADVERTISE CONTACT Jenny Shramenko 0171 704 9776

Granta US, 1755 Broadway, 5th Floor, New York, NY 10019-3780, USA

PUBLISHER Rea S. Hederman

SUBSCRIPTION DETAILS: a one-year subscription (four issues) costs £24.95 (UK), £32.95 (rest of Europe) and £39.95 (rest of the world).

Granta is printed in the United States of America. The paper used in this publication meets the minimum requirements of American National Standard for Information Sciences—Permanence of Paper for Printed Library Materials, ANSI Z39.48-1984. ∞

Granta is published by Granta Publications and distributed in the United Kingdom by Bloomsbury, 38 Soho Square, London W1V 5DF, and in the United States by Penguin Books USA Inc, 375 Hudson Street, New York, NY 10014, USA. This selection copyright © 1997 Granta Publications.

Cover design by The Senate
Cover photograph: Getty Images

ISBN 0 903141 10 8

FINBAR'S HOTEL

During the course of one night, Finbar's Hotel is visited by a bewildering array of guests . . .

a novel by

DERMOT BOLGER • RODDY DOYLE

ANNE ENRIGHT • HUGO HAMILTON

JENNIFER JOHNSTON • JOSEPH O'CONNOR

COLM TÓIBÍN

A Picador Paperback Original

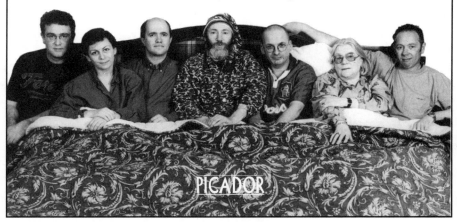

PICADOR

F R A N C E

ECM NEW SERIES

JEAN-LUC GODARD
NOUVELLE VAGUE

The complete soundtrack - music, dialogue, sounds - of Jean-Luc Godard's Nouvelle Vague, premiered at the Cannes Film Festival in 1990. With music by Dino Saluzzi, David Darling, Paul Hindemith, Arnold Schoenberg, Paul Giger, Patti Smith, Meredith Monk, Heinz Holliger, Werner Pirchner, and the voices of Alain Delon, Domiziana Giordano, Roland Amstutz and Laurence Cote.

"The Nouvelle Vague soundtrack is magnificent. The intertwining of the various forms of music, voices and sounds is one of the most extraordinary ever heard, even including Godard's oeuvre."
Cahiers du Cinéma

ECM New Series 1600/01
4498912 2CD set

The ECM New Series Catalogue is available from selected retailers or write to
New Note, Electron House, Cray Avenue, Orpington, Kent BR5 3RJ

ECM Records, Postfach 600331, 81203 Munich www.ecmrecords.com

EDITORIAL

The first man to fly solo across the Atlantic and the hero of his age, Charles Lindbergh, saw France from the air on 21 May 1927. He had been flying for more than thirty hours and seen nothing but ocean since he left New York, and now the green fields and woods of Normandy were below him. Journey's end! Time for a bite! He took a sandwich from its wrapper and stretched to throw the wrapper from the cockpit. Then he looked down and decided that just wouldn't do. 'My first act,' Lindbergh said to himself, 'will not be to sully such a beautiful garden.' His American waste paper remained in the aircraft—scrunched, one assumes, in a ball at his feet.

The French writer Jean-Marie Domenach, who died this summer, tells this story in his last book: *Regarder la France—Essai sur le Malaise française*. It is for Domenach yet another small stone in a large mountain of anecdotal evidence gathered to demonstrate the singularity of France as a state, a people, a culture and (in this case) a landscape. But, as Domenach's subtitle indicates, all isn't well with this singularity. The fields that Lindbergh flew over are larger now, the roads straighter and wider, the peasants (should Lindbergh have spotted any, bending their backs in this beautiful garden) dramatically fewer. All of these changes have happened to most other western countries as agriculture has adopted new machines and new techniques to plough out hedges and plough in chemical fertilizers, to relegate agricultural labourers to models in museums of folklore. But in none of these other countries (even England, where the countryside supplies a large part of the national idea) would rural transformation be seen as such a blow to the nation's identity. There would be nostalgia, of course, and ecological concern. In France, things go much further. Implied in Domenach's story is the notion that, had Lindbergh been flying over some other, less top-quality country (Portugal, say, or Belgium), he might have nonchalantly tossed the paper into the windstream and had a good spit at the same time. But, as General and President Charles de Gaulle was fond of saying, France is . . . France. Even Lindbergh, high up in his frail aeroplane, and with a hundred other things to worry about, could see the specialness of the place and respect it.

Nobody doubts that France is special; certainly not the French. It is the largest, though not the most populous country, in Europe, and was once the most powerful. Its linguistic unity and its natural boundaries—France can be seen as a hexagonal fortress with sea on three sides and mountains on two—have given it a clearer identity, a less contested nationalism, than most countries which share a continent. Its history is alive with symbols, events, heroes and slogans which have not been shuttered in to the cobwebbed past—which form part of France's grand and still unfolding story, as the French tell it to themselves. France

7

sees itself as the birthplace of modern ideas and modern politics. The words of the American constitution are fine, but a snappier political credo than 'Liberty, Equality, Fraternity' has still to be invented. The terms 'Left' and 'Right' as in left-wing and right-wing come from the seating arrangements in the National Assembly of 1789, when the pro-revolutionaries took the benches on the left side of the chamber. When Britain was manufacturing industrial and necessarily temporary objects, France was taking the lead in creating enduring, and now universal, abstractions. These ideals, which have dignified humankind, form part of France's claim to its status as a universal nation. Add them to a cultural pre-eminence which has lasted through most of the last and the present century—think of the French novel and French painting in the nineteenth, French film in the twentieth—and a way of living notorious for its discriminating pleasure in philosophy, love, food, drink and fashion, and France's claim to be the global model for civilization can seem unanswerable. 'Ah, the French,' as the maxim goes on the northbound Channel ferry and the jet heading west to North America, 'they know how to *live!*'

The paradox is that, while France has thought of itself as a tutor to the world, it has never really believed that it can be imitated. France is distinctive. It may believe, as the USA affects to believe (or simply assumes), that it is a country with values which can be franchised anywhere; but unlike perfumes, croissants and fizzy water—unlike, in fact, the Statue of Liberty—some items are not for export. There is the French soul; there is an even mistier item, *la France profonde*. Here normal rules do not apply. Sooner or later, in almost every area of human activity, one comes across the phrase: *l'exception française*. Exceptionally, France has retained several parts of its empire with little sense of post-imperial shame. Exceptionally, in the 1990s it began again to explode nuclear devices under one of these old outposts (when on British television a French government spokesman was asked why, if these tests were so safe, they were not conducted under French waters rather than in the far-away Pacific, he replied: 'But Tahiti *is* France'). Exceptionally, it still regards French as the near-rival to English as the triumphant world language, when nearly four times as many people speak English (and three times as many use Spanish, and twice as many Bengali—or Arabic). Exceptionally, it is the most anti-American country in western (or for that matter eastern) Europe.

Nearly all of these exceptions flow from what is now the greatest exception of all: the power of the French state to regulate, subsidize, satisfy and inspire the lives and ambitions of France's fifty-eight million citizens. The urge to standardize and centralize in France predates the Revolution, but it was the precepts of the Revolution, later codified by

Napoleon, which allowed French citizens to feel that they played equal parts in a grand and unifying design. There would be standard courts dispensing standard law, standard schools teaching the same French history, standard forms of local administration sitting in headquarters with *Liberté, Egalité, Fraternité* standardly engraved in their stone. The language would be standard despite its many regional variants, the measurements (metres, litres, kilos) also. All standards would be set by the government in Paris. The state interfered but it also sheltered, and it became one of the glories of France, inseparable from the idea of the French way of life. Today France employs five million civil servants (proportionately five times as many as the USA) and industries run by the state comprise more than a third of the French economy.

The state, then, matters in France as it does in few other countries. It has never been, unlike in Britain or the USA, the bogey of the tax-paying middle classes. For one thing, it keeps a large part of the middle class in work; more than half the families in France depend on income from the state. For another, its regulations and subsidies have sustained the attractive variousnesses of France, which still produces four hundred (or a thousand; the boast varies) different kinds of cheese, and where a town of 1,700 people can contain (this is a real but typical example, from Beaujolais) three bakeries, a butcher, two grocers, a pharmacy, a jeweller's, two clothes shops, a flower shop, two hardware stores, a newsagent, two garages, several bars, two hotels and two restaurants, one of which is mentioned honourably in the Michelin guide. In Britain and North America, supermarkets and shopping malls would have closed most of them, while politicians spoke airily about the free market's great virtue of consumer choice.

But—re-enter *le malaise française*—unemployment runs at 12.5 per cent (double the British figure) and the centralized political and bureaucratic elites of Paris have become deeply unpopular and sometimes corrupt. And the nation state is now retreating throughout the world as a custodian of economies and cultures, abandoning its old remits to the capricious pressures of the global market. France has many phrases for this phenomenon—*le capitalisme sauvage, le capitalisme dur* (hard), *le capitalisme Anglo-Saxon*—and most of them could be heard in the elections of June this year, when France ditched its right-wing government and replaced it with an alliance of Socialists and Communists. On the face of it, the Left had capitalized on France's prevailing moods of *sinistrose* (dismalness) and *morosité* (gloom) by promising that the two great forces for change in French life could be resisted: that France needn't bow to Chinese wage rates or cut its public spending so that it could qualify for membership of European Monetary

Union. The Left pledged that it would create 700,000 jobs, half of them funded by the state, and cut the statutory working week from forty to thirty-five hours with no reduction in earnings. In Britain, where Mrs Thatcher expunged socialism from the politics of her Labour successors, there was mockery and also half a cheer.

France was being exceptional once again, struggling to preserve its cherished ideas of Frenchness. To the rest of the world, which has accepted globalism as an inevitability, the way things are and will be, it seemed as though its fourth-largest economy had recoiled in the face of modernity; that Fortress France was pulling up the drawbridge.

Where does French writing stand in all this? The awkward truth here is that, outside France and small pockets of Francophilia, hardly anyone knows. Name six living French novelists. Name six contemporary French novels. The French, of course, blame this neglect on Anglo-Saxon ignorance and hostility, but the truth (our truth, at least) is that, in literature, France pulled up the drawbridge long ago. Saul Bellow, writing in *Granta* in 1984, remembered how Paris had been the capital of international culture before the Second World War and how, on his first visit in 1948, the city had still seemed 'one of the permanent settings, a theatre if you like, where the greatest problems of existence might be represented.' Thirty years later that feeling had gone. 'Marxism, Euro-communism, Existentialism, Structuralism, Deconstructionism could not restore the potency of French civilization,' Bellow wrote. 'Sorry about that.'

It would be unwise to discount this as a prejudiced American view. Jean-Marie Domenach in his book *Regarder la France*, published this year, describes what we have come to think of as typical French writing in terms that are forbiddingly recognizable to anyone who has struggled with the Noveau Roman: 'Cold descriptions of society which have become affluent and disintegrated, where individuals float like children's balloons in joyless streets, unconscious of their destiny and locked in a perpetual present.' Domenach notes that there have been few 'social' novels, and that nothing great has come from the dramatic French experiences of withdrawal from Indo-China and Algeria. He blames consumerism, the rise of television, and the retreat from society into private life, but as none of these are peculiar to France (and have probably had a much larger effect in Britain and the USA), it can't be the full explanation. How could a literature which perfected the realistic, spacious (and popular) novel of the nineteenth century—Balzac, Flaubert, Zola—turn a hundred years later to the perfection of introspective, narrow (and unpopular) novels which seek only to demonstrate the essential solitude and meaninglessness of existence?

10

Bellow may have some of the answers: Existentialism, Structuralism etc. have had an unsteadying and often shrivelling effect on the act of authorship, whatever they have achieved in linguistics and anthropology. But there may be others. Solitude may be to blame. Proust may be to blame. It was Proust who raised introspection to an epic height and made it seem, to many who came after him, the only true subject for literature. This self-importance on the page is allied to the public importance accorded to writers in France, where the winner of the Prix Goncourt can sell a million copies (though the cry heard in bookshops, *Donnez-moi Le Goncourt!* suggests that buyers may be disciples of fashion rather than literature). Too often, in novel after novel, the result is that writers seem merely to be pointing out that the world is too crude and insensitive to recognize and reward their own delicate temperament.

Or that at least *was* the situation. Today in France there are arguments about the purpose of writing and a movement to put the world back into the book; it hasn't escaped the French that the failure of French writing to sell abroad may have, to put it strictly in terms of the market, more to do with the producer than the consumer. Today a younger generation of writers is emerging which is more willing to look outward again. Many of these writers come from present or former French territories outside Europe, or are the children of migrants from those places. This issue of *Granta* contains a memory from Patrick Chamoiseau of his boyhood in Martinique, and a story, a true one, from Assia Djebar, who has an Algerian father and a French (European) mother. Some are French only by language. Caroline Lamarche, also in this issue, is a Belgian citizen who publishes in Paris. What their writing has in common is the desire to dramatize the deed rather than the thought, the story above the idea.

They reflect a France that is richer and more complicated than the beleaguered monolith of newspaper headlines, and which cannot be accommodated by old ideas of Frenchness, no matter what its government may say or do. France, we should never forget, has the largest Muslim community in Europe, between three and five million people, and Europe's largest Jewish community (about 700,000 people) outside Russia. A third of France's population has ancestry from outside its borders.

Beneath the crust of its mythology, France has already changed. Why otherwise would Jean-Marie Le Pen and his anti-immigrant, anti-Europe, anti-American party, the National Front, exist? And why in June would they have won fifteen per cent of the vote? The real challenge to France is not the Anglo-Saxon world. It is to find a new and more plural identity, freed from the burden of glorious memory. ☐

RICHARD FORD

WOMEN WITH MEN

"Richard Ford has throughout his work acknowledged the central importance that women and marriage have in the lives of men. He has had the originality - the strength - to bend the Hemingway tradition to his own use rather than discard its troubled legacy. Nobody now writing... looks more like an American classic"

Michael Gorra, *New York Times Book Review*

GRANTA

MICHEL HOUELLEBECQ
WE ARE THE KINGS

The problem is, it's just not enough to live by the rules. Sure, you manage to live by them. Sometimes it's tight, extremely tight, but on the whole you manage. Your tax papers are up to date. Your invoices paid on time. You never go out without your identity card (and the special little wallet for your Visa!).

And yet you haven't any friends.

What's to be done? How do you use your time? In dedicating yourself to helping others? But basically other folk don't interest you. Listening to records? It used to be a solution, but as the years go by you have to say that music moves you less and less.

Taken in its widest sense, a spot of do-it-yourself can be a way out. But the fact is nothing can halt the ever-increasing recurrence of those moments when your total isolation, the sensation of an all-consuming emptiness, the foreboding that your existence is nearing a painful and disastrous end, all combine to plunge you into a state of real suffering.

And yet you haven't always wanted to die.

You have had a life. There have been moments when you were having a life. Of course you don't remember too much about it; but there are photographs to prove it. This was probably occurring around the time of your adolescence, or just after. How great your appetite for life was then! Existence seemed rich in possibilities. You might become a pop singer, go off to Venezuela.

More surprising still, you have had a childhood. Observe, now, a child of seven, playing with his little soldiers on the living-room carpet. Please observe him closely. Since the divorce he no longer has a father. Only rarely does he see his mother, who occupies an important post in a cosmetics firm. Nevertheless, he plays with his little soldiers and the interest he takes in these representations of the world and of war seems very keen. He already lacks a bit of affection, that's for sure, but what an air he has of being interested in the world!

You too have been interested in the world. That was long ago. I ask you to cast your mind back to then. The world of rules was no longer enough for you; you had to enter into the world of struggle. I ask you to go back to that precise moment. It was long ago, wasn't it? Cast your mind back: the water was cold.

You are far from the edge, now. Oh yes! How far from the

edge you are! You long believed in the existence of another bank: that is no longer the case. You go on swimming, though, and every movement you make brings you closer to drowning. You are suffocating, your lungs are on fire. The water seems colder and colder to you, less and less of a joke. You aren't that young any more. Now you are going to die. It's nothing. I am here. I won't let you sink. Go on with your reading.

Cast your mind back once more to your introduction to the world of struggle.

I've just turned thirty. After a chaotic start I did very well in my studies. Today I'm in middle management. Analyst-programmer in a computer software company, my salary is two and a half times the national average: by any standard a tidy purchasing power. I can expect significant advancement within my firm. Unless I decide, as many do, to sign on with a client. All in all I may consider myself satisfied with my social status. On the sexual plane, on the other hand, the success is less resounding. I have had many women, but for limited periods. Lacking in looks as well as personal charm, subject to frequent bouts of depression, I don't in the least correspond to what women are usually looking for in a man. And then I've always felt a kind of slight reticence with women who were opening themselves to me. Basically all I represented for them was a last resort. Not, you will agree, the ideal point of departure for a lasting relationship.

Since my break-up with Véronique, two years ago, I haven't known any woman in fact. The feeble and inconsistent attempts I've made in that direction have only resulted in predictable failure. Two years is a long time. But in reality, above all when one is working, it's no time at all. Anyone will tell you: it's no time at all.

I generally see nobody at the weekends. I stay home, do a bit of tidying. I get pleasantly depressed.

This Saturday, however, between eight and eleven, there's a social engagement in the offing. I am to eat with a friend, a priest, in a Mexican restaurant. The restaurant is good; on that front, no problem. But is my friend still my friend?

15

We did our studies together. We were twenty, just kids really. Now we're thirty. Once he'd got his engineer's diploma he went off to the seminary, he changed course. Today he's a parish priest in Vitry. It isn't an easy parish.

I eat a red-bean taco and Jean-Pierre Buvet talks to me about sex. According to him, the interest our society pretends to show in eroticism (through advertising, magazines, the media in general) is artificial. In reality most people are quickly bored by the subject, but they feign the opposite out of a bizarre inverted hypocrisy.

He gets to his main thesis. Our civilization, he says, suffers from vital exhaustion. In the century of Louis XIV, when the appetite for living was great, official culture placed the accent on the negation of pleasure and of the flesh; insistently repeated that worldly life can offer only imperfect joys, that the only true source of happiness was in God. Such a discourse, he declares, would no longer be tolerated today. We need adventure and eroticism because we need to hear ourselves repeat that life is marvellous and exciting; and it's manifestly clear that we rather doubt this.

I get the impression he considers me a fitting symbol of this vital exhaustion. No sex drive, no ambition; no real interests. I can only reply that I get the impression everybody's a bit like that. I consider myself a normal person. Well, perhaps not completely, but who is completely, huh? Eighty per cent normal, let's say.

For something to say in the meantime I casually observe that these days everybody is bound, at one moment or another in his life, to have the feeling of being a failure. We are agreed on that.

The conversation gets bogged down. I nibble my caramelized vermicelli. He advises me to find God again, or to enter psychoanalysis; I give a start at the comparison. He's interested in my case, he explains. He seems to think I'm in a bad way. I'm isolated, far too isolated. According to him it isn't natural.

We have a cognac. He lays his cards on the table. As far as he's concerned Jesus is the answer, the wellspring of life. Of a rich and active life. 'You must accept your divine nature!' he exclaims. The next table turns round. I feel a little tired. I have the impression we're arriving at an impasse. I smile, just in case. I haven't too many friends, and don't want to lose this one. 'You must accept your divine nature,' he repeats more softly. I promise

I'll make an effort. I add a few more phrases, I force myself to re-establish a consensus.

Next, a coffee, and then each to his home. In the end it was a good evening.

On getting to work on Monday, I learned that my company had just sold a specialized software program to the Ministry of Agriculture and that I'd been chosen to train them to use it. Long before the word became fashionable, my company developed an authentic enterprise culture (the creation of a logo, distribution of sweatshirts to the salaried staff, motivation seminars in Turkey). It's a top-flight firm, enjoying an enviable reputation in its field. A nice little number all round. I can't walk out just like that, you understand.

I made an appointment at the Ministry of Agriculture with a girl called Catherine Lechardoy. The specialized software program itself was called 'Maple'. The Maple program was to be used for paying government subsidies to the farmers, an area Catherine Lechardoy was responsible for, at the data processing level that is. Up till now we'd never met, Catherine Lechardoy and I. In short, this was a 'first contact'.

As it happened Catherine Lechardoy wasn't there when I showed up in room 6017. She'd been, I was told, 'held up by a debugging on the central site'. I was invited to take a seat and wait for her, which I did. The conversation revolved around an outrage that had taken place the evening before on the Champs-Elysées. A bomb had been planted under a seat in a café. Two people were dead. A third had had her legs and half her face torn off; she'd be maimed and blind for life. I learned that this wasn't the first such outrage. A few days earlier a bomb had exploded in a post office near the Hôtel de Ville, blowing a fifty-year-old woman to bits. I also learned that these bombs were planted by Arab terrorists, who were demanding the release of other Arab terrorists, held in France for various killings.

By five, Catherine Lechardoy still hadn't returned, so I left. The 'first contact' would happen some other day, I guessed.

I'm told next morning that I've made a faux pas. I should have insisted on seeing Catherine Lechardoy. My unexplained departure has been taken badly by the Ministry of Agriculture.

I also learn—and this is a complete surprise—that since my last contract my work has not given complete satisfaction. They'd said nothing up to now, but I had been found wanting. With this Ministry of Agriculture contract I am, to some extent, being offered a second chance. My head of department assumes a tense air, pure soap opera, when telling me, 'We're at the service of the client, you know. In our line of business, alas, it's rare to get a second chance.'

I regret making this man unhappy. He is very handsome. A face at once sensual and manly, with close-cut grey hair. White shirt of an impeccable fine weave, allowing some powerful and bronzed pecs to show through. Club tie. Natural and decisive movements, indicative of a perfect physical condition.

The only excuse I can come up with—and it seems extremely feeble to me, though it is true—is that my car has just been stolen. My head of department flips. The theft of my car visibly angers him. He didn't know, couldn't have guessed. Now he gets it. And when the moment for leavetaking comes, standing by the door of his office, feet planted in the thick pearl-grey moquette, it's with emotion that he urges me to 'hang in there'.

The following morning I meet the head of the Ministry of Agriculture 'Computer Studies' section. He seems to have given himself the mission of embodying an exaggerated version of the young and dynamic boss. In this he's streets ahead of anything I've had occasion to observe up till now. His shirt is open, as if he hadn't quite had the time to button it up, and his tie off to one side as if caught in a slipstream. He doesn't walk down the corridors, he glides. If he could fly, he would. His face is shining, his hair disordered and damp as if he'd come straight from the swimming pool.

He places his hand on my shoulder and speaks in a gentle voice, saying how much he's sorry for making me wait for nothing the other day. I give him an angelic smile, tell him it's of no importance, that I understand, and know that sooner or later the meeting will take place. I am being sincere. It is a very tender moment. He is leaning towards me and me alone. You'd think we were two lovers whom life has just reunited after a long absence.

The next day I learn that a sophisticated three-tier system of training has been set in place by the Ministry (therefore by him, if I understand aright). It is a question of how best to respond to the needs of the users by means of a complementary but organically independent package of training programmes. It clearly bears the stamp of a subtle mind.

In real terms, it means that I will be involved in a tour that will take me firstly to Rouen for two weeks, then to Dijon for a week, and lastly to La Roche-sur-Yon for four days. I will leave on 1 December and be home again for Christmas, to 'spend the holiday with my family'. The human aspect has not been forgotten, then. How splendid.

The next day I went to a farewell drink for someone at the Ministry of Agriculture. Catherine Lechardoy was there too. The object of this moment of conviviality was a small man of some sixty years with grey hair and thick glasses. The staff had clubbed together to buy him a fishing rod—a high-performance Japanese job, with three-speed reel and range modifiable by simple finger pressure—but he didn't know this yet. He was staying well in sight beside the bottles of champagne. People were coming up and giving him a friendly pat on the back, even evoking a shared memory.

Catherine Lechardoy had red on her mouth and blue on her eyes. Her skirt reached halfway down her thighs and her tights were black. The hubbub in the room became slightly more animated. I imagined her in Galeries Lafayette choosing a Brazilian tanga, a bikini in scarlet lace. I felt consumed by an aching sense of compassion.

A clear silence fell. Then, seeking a way out of the impasse, she proceeded to talk about the streamlining of work procedures between the servicing company and the Ministry—that's to say, between the two of us. She was still right beside me—our bodies were separated by a gap of thirty centimetres at most—when she lightly rubbed the bias of my jacket collar between her fingers.

19

I felt no desire for Catherine Lechardoy. She was looking at me and smiling, drinking Crémant, trying her hardest to be brave. After my third glass I came close to suggesting we leave together, go and fuck in some office. On the desk or on the carpet, it didn't matter; I was feeling up to making the necessary gestures. But I kept quiet, and anyway I don't think she'd have said yes. Or rather I would first have had to put my arm around her waist, say she was beautiful, brush her lips in a tender kiss. There was nothing to be done, it was clear.

A gloomy week. We were at the end of November, a time which is generally taken to be gloom itself. For me it seemed normal that, for want of more tangible events, the changes in the weather might assume a certain place in my life. Anyway, that's all old people talk about these days, I'm told.

I've lived so little that I have a tendency to imagine that I'm not going to die. It seems improbable that human existence can be reduced to so little. One can't help but imagine that sooner or later something is bound to happen. A big mistake. A life can quite easily be both empty and short. The days slip by, leaving neither trace nor memory. And then all of a sudden they stop.

Maybe, I tell myself, this tour of the provinces is going to alter my ideas. Probably negatively, but it is going to alter my ideas. At least there will be a change of direction, a shake-up.

We're talking Monday morning, 1 December. It is cold and I am waiting for Tisserand by the departure gate of the train for Rouen. We're talking the Gare Saint-Lazare. I'm getting colder and colder and more and more pissed off. My colleague, Tisserand, arrives at the last minute. We're going to have difficulty finding seats, unless he's got himself a first-class ticket; that would be quite his style.

I might have formed a twosome with any one of four or five people from my company, and in the end it's come down to Tisserand. I'm not wildly excited about it. He, on the other hand, declares himself delighted. 'You and me, we make a fantastic team,' he tells me straight away, 'I reckon it's gonna work out great.' He describes a sort of rotating movement with his hands, as if to symbolize our future understanding.

Tisserand and I have chatted many a time around the hot-drinks machine. He mostly told dirty stories. I have the feeling this tour of the provinces is going to be grim.

We skirt the Seine, scarlet, completely drowned in the rays of the rising sun—one really could think the river gorged with blood.

Our first evening in Rouen consists, to begin with, of finding a hotel. On Tisserand's initiative we book into the Armes Cauchoises. A good hotel, a very good hotel; and anyway our expenses are reimbursed, right?

Next he wants to have an aperitif. By all means!

In the café he chooses a table not far from two girls. He sits down, the girls get up and go. No doubt about it, the plan is perfectly synchronized. Bravo girls, bravo!

In desperation he orders a Martini. I content myself with a beer. I don't stop smoking, I light one cigarette after another.

He tells me he's just signed on with a gym to lose a bit of weight, 'and also to score, of course'. That's hunkydory, I've nothing against it.

I realize I'm smoking more and more; I must be on at least four packs a day. Smoking cigarettes has become the only element of real freedom in my day-to-day existence. The only act to which I tenaciously cling with my whole being. My only project.

Tisserand next broaches a favourite theme of his, namely that 'it's us guys, the computer experts, who are the kings'. I suppose by that he means a high salary, a certain professional status, a great facility for changing jobs. And OK, within these limits he isn't wrong. We are the kings.

He develops the notion. I open my fifth pack of Camels. Shortly afterwards he finishes his Martini. He wants to go back to the hotel to change for dinner. OK, fine, let's do it.

I wait for him in the lounge while watching television. There's something on about student demonstrations. One of these, in Paris, has assumed enormous proportions: according to the journalists there were at least 300,000 people on the streets. It was supposed to be a non-violent demonstration, more like a big party. And like all non-violent demonstrations it turned nasty: a student has lost an eye, a riot policeman has had a hand torn off, etc.

Tisserand returns; he has put on a sort of evening shell-suit, black and gold, which makes him look rather like a scarab beetle. OK, let's do it.

At my insistence we go to the Flunch. It's a place where you can eat chips with an unlimited quantity of mayonnaise (all you do is scoop as much mayonnaise as you want from a giant bucket). I'd be quite happy with a plate of chips drowned in mayonnaise, and a beer. But Tisserand immediately orders a couscous royal and a bottle of Sidi Brahim. After the second glass of wine he begins eyeing up the waitresses, the customers, anybody. Sad young man. Sad, sad young man. I'm well aware of why he likes my company so much: it's because I never speak of my girlfriends, I never make a big thing of my female conquests. And so he feels justified in supposing (rightly, as it happens) that for one reason or another I don't have a sex life; and for him that's one less burden, a slight lessening of his own tribulations.

After the meal he wants to go for a drink in a 'nice' café. Wonderful.

I follow just behind, and I have to say that this time his choice turns out to be excellent: we go into a kind of huge vaulted cellar, with old, obviously authentic beams. Small wooden tables, lit with candles, are dotted all over the place. A fire burns in an immense fireplace at the end of the room. The whole effect creates an atmosphere of happy improvisation, of congenial disorder.

We sit down. He orders a bourbon and water, I stick to beer. I look about me and think to myself that this is the place, that maybe this will prove a happy hunting ground for my luckless companion. We're in a student café, everyone's happy, everybody wants to have fun. There are lots of tables with two or three young women at them; there are even some women alone at the bar.

Assuming my most engaging air, I watch Tisserand. The young men and women in the café touch each other. The women push back their hair with a graceful gesture. They cross their legs, await the right time to burst into laughter. After all, they're having fun. Now's the time for flirting. This is it, at this precise moment, in this place which lends itself so perfectly.

He raises his eyes from his drink and, from behind his glasses, rests his gaze on me. And I perceive that he's run out of steam. He can't go on, he has no more appetite for the fray, he's had it up to here. He looks at me, his face trembles a little. Doubtless it's the alcohol, he drank too much wine at dinner, the idiot. I wonder if he isn't going to break into sobs, recount the stations of his particular cross to me. I sense that he is ready for something of the sort. The lenses of his glasses are slightly fogged with tears.

It's not a problem, I can handle it, listen to the lot, carry him back to the hotel if I have to. But I'm sure that come tomorrow morning he'll be pissed off with me.

I keep mum. I wait, saying nothing. I find no judicious words to utter. The uncertainty persists for a minute or so, then the crisis passes. In a strangely feeble, almost trembling voice he says to me: 'We'd best go back. Have to begin first thing in the morning.'

Right, we'll be off. We'll finish our drinks and we'll be off. I light a last cigarette, look at Tisserand once more. He's well and truly whacked. Wordlessly he lets me pay the bill, wordlessly he follows me as I make for the door. He's stooped, huddled. He's ashamed of himself, hates himself, wishes he were dead.

We walk in the direction of the hotel. In the street it's starting to rain. That's it then, our first day in Rouen is over. And I know, on this evidence, that the days ahead will be rigorously identical.

I don't know why, but I've decided to stay in Rouen this weekend. Tisserand was astonished to hear it. I explained to him I wanted to see the town and that I had nothing better to do in Paris. I don't really want to see the town.

And yet there are very fine medieval remains, some ancient houses of great charm. Five or six centuries ago Rouen must have been one of the most beautiful towns in France, but now everything is fucked. Everything is dirty, grimy, run down, ruined by the abiding presence of cars, noise, pollution. I don't know who the mayor is, but it only takes ten minutes of walking the streets of the old town to realize that he is totally incompetent, or corrupt. To make matters worse there are dozens of yobs who roar down the streets on their motorbikes or scooters, and without silencers. They come in from the Rouen suburbs, which are nearing total industrial collapse. Their objective is to make a deafening racket, the most disagreeable possible for the local residents. In this they are completely successful.

I leave my hotel around two. Without thinking, I go in the direction of the place du Vieux Marché. It is a truly vast square, bordered entirely by cafés, restaurants and luxury shops. It's here that Joan of Arc was burnt more than 500 years ago. To commemorate the event they've piled up a load of weirdly curved concrete slabs, half stuck in the ground, which turn out on closer inspection to be a church. I settle myself on one of the slabs, determined to get to the bottom of things. It seems highly likely that this square is the heart, the central nucleus of the town. What game is being played here exactly?

I notice that all these people seem satisfied with themselves and the universe; it's astonishing, even a little frightening. They quietly saunter around, this one displaying a quizzical smile, that one a moronic look. Some of the youngsters are dressed in leather jackets with slogans on the back borrowed from the more primitive kind of hard rock: KILL THEM ALL! or FUCK AND DESTROY! But all come together in the certainty of passing an agreeable afternoon primarily devoted to consumerism, and thus to the consolidation of their being.

I observe that I feel different to them, without, however, being able to define the nature of this difference.

The next evening I took ill. After dinner Tisserand wanted to go on to a club; I declined the invitation. My left shoulder was hurting me and I was racked by shivering. Returning to the hotel, I tried to sleep but it was no good. Once stretched out I was unable to breathe. I sat up again. The wallpaper was depressing.

An hour later I started having difficulty breathing, even sitting up. I went over to the sink. My colour was cadaverous. The pain had begun its slow descent from the shoulder towards the heart. That's when I remarked to myself that my condition was perhaps serious. I'd clearly overdone the cigarettes of late.

I stayed leaning against the sink for some twenty minutes, feeling the pain getting worse and worse. It vexed me greatly to go out again, to go to the hospital, all that.

Around one in the morning I banged the door shut and went

out. By now the pain was localized in the region of the heart. Each breath cost me an enormous effort, and manifested itself as a muffled wheezing. I was scarcely able to walk, except by taking tiny steps, one foot at a time. I was continually obliged to lean against the cars.

I rested for a few minutes against a Peugeot 104, then began the ascent of a street that appeared to lead to a more important crossroads. It took me around half an hour to cover 450 yards. The pain had stopped getting worse, yet went on being intense. On the other hand my difficulty in breathing was becoming more and more serious, and that was most alarming. I had the feeling that if this continued I was going to die within the next few hours, before dawn anyway. The injustice of such a sudden death hit me. I could hardly be said to have abused life. For a few years I was, it's true, in a bit of a bad way. But that wasn't sufficient reason for cutting short the experience. What's more, this town and its inhabitants had been instantly repugnant to me. Not only did I not want to die, but above all I did not want to die in Rouen. To die in Rouen, in the midst of the Rouennais, was a particularly odious thought. That would be, I told myself, in a state of slight delirium probably engendered by pain, to accord them too great an honour, these idiot Rouennais.

Finally I spot an unhoped-for taxi. I try to seem blasé when announcing that I want to go to the hospital, but it doesn't really work, and the driver comes close to refusing. Even so the pathetic creep has the gall to say to me, just before moving off, that he 'hopes I won't soil his seat covers'. I've heard it said that pregnant women face the same problem when going into labour: aside from a few Cambodians, all the taxi-drivers refuse to take them for fear of finding themselves lumbered with discharges on their back seat.

So, let's go!

Once in the hospital, it has to be said, the formalities are brief. An intern looks after me, makes me do a whole series of tests. He wants, I think, to be sure I'm not going to die on him within the next hour. When the examination is finished he comes over to me and announces that I have a pericardial, and not an infarction as he'd first thought. He informs me that the early symptoms are exactly the same; but unlike the infarction, which is often fatal, the pericardial is completely benign, not the kind of thing you die of. 'You must have been scared,' he says. So as not to complicate things I reply that yes, I was; but in fact I wasn't in the least bit scared, I just had the feeling I was about to peg out at any moment. That's different.

Next I'm wheeled into the emergency ward. Once sitting on the bed I start sobbing. That helps a little. I'm alone in the ward, I don't have to hold back. Now and then a nurse pokes her head round the door, assures herself that my sobbing remains more or less constant, and goes away again.

Dawn breaks. A drunk is conveyed to the bed next to mine. I continue sobbing quietly, regularly.

One soon gets used to hospital. For a whole week I was really seriously ill. I didn't want to move or to speak. The people around me chatted to each other about their illnesses with the febrile interest that seems somewhat improper to those in good health. Nobody was complaining, in any case. All had an air of being rather satisfied with their lot, despite the far-from-natural way of life being forced on them. Despite, too, the danger hanging over them. Because at the end of the day the life of most of the patients on a cardiology ward is at risk.

I remember this fifty-five-year-old worker, it was his sixth stay: he greeted everyone, the doctor, the nurses . . . He was visibly delighted to be there. And yet here was a man who in his private life was extremely active: he was always fixing up his house, doing his garden, etc. I saw his wife, she seemed very nice. They were rather touching in their way, loving each other like that at fifty-odd. But the moment he arrived in hospital he abdicated all responsibility. He placed his body, delightedly, in the hands of science. Some day or other he would be staying for keeps in this hospital, that was clear. I can see him now, addressing the doctor with a kind of gluttonous impatience, dropping in the odd familiar abbreviation which I didn't understand: 'You're gonna do my pneumo and my venous cath then?' Oh yes, he swore by his venous cath; he talked about it every single day.

I was conscious, by comparison, of being a rather difficult patient. In point of fact I was experiencing a certain difficulty in getting a grip on myself. It's a strange experience to see one's legs as separate objects, way off from one's mind, with which they would be reunited more or less by chance, and badly at that. To imagine oneself, incredulously, as a heap of twitching limbs.

Tisserand came to see me twice; he has been wonderful, he brought me books and pastries. He really wanted to cheer me up; I knew that, so I listed some books for him. But I didn't really fancy reading. My mind was drifting, hazy, somewhat perplexed.

He made a few erotic wisecracks about the nurses, but that was inevitable, quite natural, and I bore him no grudge. Plus it's a fact that, what with the room temperatures, the nurses were usually half-naked beneath their uniforms; just a bra and pants, easily visible through their light clothing. This undeniably maintains a slight but constant erotic tension, all the more so since they are touching you, one is oneself almost naked, etc. And the sick body still wants for sensual pleasure, alas. If the truth be told, I say this as something of an afterthought. I was myself in a state of almost total erotic insensitivity, at least for the first week.

I really got the feeling the nurses and the other patients were surprised I didn't receive more visits. So I explained, for their general edification, that I was on a professional visit to Rouen at the moment it all happened. This wasn't my home town, I didn't know a soul. In short, I was there by chance.

Nevertheless, wasn't there anybody I wanted to get in touch with, inform about my state? Well no, there wasn't anybody.

The second week was harder. I was starting to get better, to manifest the desire to leave. Life was looking up again, as they say. Tisserand was no longer around to bring me pastries. By then he was already busy charming the good people of Dijon.

One morning, someone telephoned from my company. It was an executive secretary who'd been given this difficult task. She had been perfect, taking all the usual precautions and assuring me that the re-establishment of my health mattered to them more than anything else, but she was nevertheless wishing to know if I would be well enough to go to La Roche-sur-Yon, as planned. I replied that I knew nothing for sure, but that it was one of my most ardent wishes. She laughed, somewhat stupidly. But then she was a very stupid woman, as I'd already observed.

I left the hospital rather sooner, I believe, than the doctors would have preferred. Generally they try and keep you in for the longest possible time so as to increase their coefficient of occupied beds. But the holiday period no doubt inclined them towards clemency. Besides, the head doctor had promised me, 'You'll be home for Christmas': those were his very words. Home—I didn't know about that; but somewhere, that's for sure.

I made my farewells to the fifty-five-year-old worker, who'd been operated on that same morning. Everything had gone very well, according to the doctors. Be that as it may, he had the look of a man whose time was running out.

His wife absolutely insisted I taste the apple tart her husband didn't have the strength to swallow. I accepted; it was delicious.

'Keep your chin up, my son!' he said to me at the moment of leavetaking. I wished him the same. He was right. It's something that can always come in useful, keeping your chin up.

Rouen–Paris. Exactly three weeks ago I was making this same journey in the opposite direction. What's changed in the meantime? Small clusters of houses are still smoking down in the valley, holding out the promise of unalloyed happiness. The grass is green. There's sunshine, with small clouds forming a contrast; the light is more that of spring. But a bit further away the earth is flooded. You can make out the slight rippling of the water between the willows; you can imagine a sticky, blackish mud into which your feet suddenly sink.

Not far off from me in the carriage a black guy listens to his Walkman while polishing off a bottle of J & B. He struts down the aisle, bottle in hand. An animal, probably dangerous. I try to avoid his gaze, which is, however, relatively friendly. An executive type, doubtless disturbed by the black man, comes and plonks himself down opposite me. What the fuck is he doing here! He should be in first class. Can they never leave you in peace?

He has a Rolex watch, a seersucker jacket. On the third finger of his left hand he wears an averagely thin wedding ring of gold. His face is squarish, frank, rather friendly. He might be around forty. On his pale cream shirt thin stripes in relief can be distinguished of a slightly darker cream. His tie is of average width. I am obliged to turn towards the landscape so as not to see him. It's odd, but it seems to me that the sun has turned red, as it was during my trip out. But I don't give much of a damn. There could be five or six red suns out there and it wouldn't make a jot of difference to the course of my meditations.

I don't like this world. I definitely do not like it. The society in which I live—advertising, computers—disgusts me. My entire work as a computer expert consists of adding to the data, the cross-checks, the criteria of rational decision-making. It has no meaning, this useless encumbering of the neurons. This world has need of everything except more information.

The arrival in Paris, as grim as ever. The leprous façades of the Pont Cardinet flats, behind which one invariably imagines retired folk agonizing alongside their cat, which is eating up half their pension in Friskies. Those weird metal structures that indecently mount each other to form a grid of overhead wires. And the inevitable advertising hoardings flashing by, gaudy and repellent. 'A gay and changing spectacle on the walls.' Bullshit. Pure fucking bullshit. □

Translation by PAUL HAMMOND

Ringleaders

ON BOXING £5.99

PURPLE HOMICIDE
Fear and Loathing on Knutsford Heath
JOHN SWEENEY
Foreword by David Soul
£9.99

RED DIRT MARIJUANA
& other tastes
'Terry Southern
is the American
writer most
capable of handling
frenzy on a
gigantic scale.'
Esquire
£6.99

HUNTER S. THOMPSON
THE FEAR AND LOATHING LETTERS VOLUME 1
THE PROUD HIGHWAY
SAGA OF A DESPERATE SOUTHERN GENTLEMAN
£20.00

A DIFFERENT COUNTRY
Photographs by John Davies

In 1973, agriculture employed twenty per cent of France's working population. In 1994, the figure was seven per cent. Villages are quieter, fields are bigger, hedgerows have disappeared. Every weekend urban families take the new autoroutes to their country homes.

The A26 near St Quentin

Cemetery near Belfort

Quelmes near Béthune

A new estate near Belfort

Nuclear power station on the Loire at Beaulieu

Elf services on the A26

Grain silos near Reims

*War memorial to the
Canadian dead, Vimy*

Imaginative
INDIGO

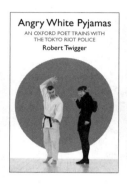

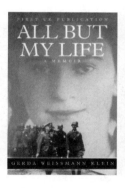

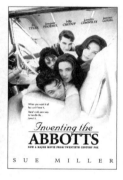

Angry White Pyjamas, *Robert Twigger* • **English Weather**, *Neil Ferguson*
Book of Two Halves, *ed. Nicholas Royle* • **All But My Life**, *Gerda Weissmann Klein*
Voice of the Fire, *Alan Moore* • **Inventing the Abbotts**, *Sue Miller*

ALL NOW AVAILABLE IN PAPERBACK

INDIGO IS AN IMPRINT OF CASSELL PLC.

ASSIA DJEBAR
A SENTENCE OF LOVE

I met Annie for the first time in 1995, in Algiers. A friend of my sister's, she came from Paris and stayed with me for one night. During the evening, as we were getting to know each other, just the two of us, Annie's story unfurled and flowered in the twilight. Back then, Algiers was still a peaceful capital, although animated by the excitement of new parties forming and recently created newspapers: 'a new political life', so people believed.

Annie needed to confide in someone. The next day she was leaving for the east of the country. She told me, simply, in muted tones, of her emotion at being able, at last, to meet Fatima, the little girl she hardly knew. 'Her' little girl.

It was an everyday story, doubtless commonplace when two countries meet. A man and a woman fall in love, and part. One of them, often the man but sometimes the woman, forcibly takes the child away, back to 'their' country, without consulting the other.

The other is helpless, and so begins a tussle against the worst of windmills—time. Time, which makes the child grow so fast, too fast, far from the sight of the dispossessed parent.

Two countries, France and Algeria, linked for so long by history in a conflict—in a union?—torn by passion, desire, violence. During the twenty or thirty years that followed the painful separation of the two national destinies, a few individuals recreated the union in the private sphere imagining that they were living out their own stories when, actually, an obscure debt was unfolding.

Some Algerian-French or French-Maghrebi marriages turn out to be well-favoured. But Annie, who had met my sister in Paris, where they had both been taking a course in Berber, was not so fortunate. She talked late into that Algiers night about the circumstances of her marriage, ten years earlier.

Newly arrived in Paris, she was a young provincial girl who had left her native Anjou. Her 'beloved', Idir, was a builder's mate, an immigrant of four or five years who lived in a hostel for single foreigners: he worked hard, saved his money to send back to Kabylia and had never approached a European woman.

Annie was the first he dared speak to—by chance, in a record shop where she was listening to a Berber lament that was popular at the time; before buying the record, she had asked what it was about. The assistant called over Idir, a neighbour who was hanging around in the shop—it was a Saturday. Annie listened as he unfolded the words of the lament, smiled at him with her huge, innocent eyes, paid for the record and said goodbye. And returned the following Saturday. Idir was the first man to whom she gave herself. 'He was so handsome and so kind!' she recalled.

Very quickly, she married him, despite her father's misgivings when she introduced her betrothed to her parents in their village.

'An Arab? Do you trust him?'

'Father, he speaks Kabyle, not Arabic!'

'It's the same thing,' grumbled her father, who did not, however, stand in their way.

They were happy for two years, despite Idir's furious jealousy over trifles. Annie generally gave in. She performed her secretarial duties, kept herself to herself, and went home to him. She became as isolated as she had been on her arrival in Paris.

Then she gave birth to a daughter, Fatima. During the following months their relationship was stormy, though with periods of tenderness and harmony. But Idir would fly into a rage for no reason.

'Probably,' admitted Annie, 'he was working too hard. But what annoyed him most was the fact that I continued to go to work, and handed my daughter over to a nanny every morning.'

'We had six months of continuous rowing,' she went on. 'And then one day I asked for a divorce. Initially, we had to separate.'

Annie paused, choked.

With the break-up, the divorce process was set in motion. Annie would raise Fatima, who was six or seven months old: naturally, she agreed to leave her with Idir on Sundays; later, he would have her during the holidays. She had no intention of keeping the girl from her father any more than was reasonable; it was just that Fatima was so little! They would see. That, at least, Annie was sure of: Idir was naturally gentle, and although he had proved to be too difficult as a husband, would certainly remain an affectionate father. Annie did not anticipate that their quarrel would worsen, and she was angry with herself for years afterwards for being so naive at the time.

Because for Idir, the divorce felt like a chasm. He was separated from his wife, of course: he still loved her and said so. But how could he bear being cut off from his daughter? She would grow up, and he would see her only on Sundays? He suddenly discovered, like a swelling abscess, that this was France, a land where fathers could not be all-powerful.

He made up his mind. After spending a couple of Sundays in dejected silence at his father-in-law's house in the village outside Anjou, he returned a fortnight later in a taxi. He asked the taxi to wait further up the road, on a bend.

He went inside. Annie smiled at him and they exchanged a few words. Annie was changing the baby's nappy. She scooped up Fatima and held her out to him, her bare bottom white with talc.

'Wait a second! I'll go and get some clean nappies and tell Father you're here!'

Her father would probably insist that Idir eat with them.

She rushed upstairs to the bathroom. The front door, near the kitchen and next to the little living room, was wide open.

On the stairs, Annie spoke to her father and came back down with the nappies. The door was still open, the living room was empty. She ventured out on to the front steps. The taxi was disappearing into the distance.

She called two or three times: 'Idir!'

Only after an hour did she finally ring her lawyer at home. She asked, still stunned, 'What should I do?' She continued to believe that Idir had taken his daughter for a walk, on impulse, 'just to spend some time alone with her'.

'With a bare bottom?' replied her father, adding: 'You'd do better to phone the police and tell them about the taxi!'

She wasted another hour, agitatedly wandering from room to room, before facing the facts: Idir had kidnapped Fatima.

For ever? No, she did not think so.

She did not sleep that night. In the morning, her lawyer decided to circulate Idir's description to the border police.

But by then Idir—who had decided to abandon everything: his job, his hostel, his plans—had already boarded the plane for Algiers. His little girl would stay with him for ever, he said to himself. He felt reassured, resolute.

Nine years passed, nearly ten. It was as if Annie was paralysed. She did not join those support groups for French mothers separated, like her, from their children. Except for attending to the divorce, which went through almost automatically, she did nothing except sign the lawyer's application for Idir to be arrested if he were to come back unexpectedly. Idir never came back. It did not take long for Annie to realize that her husband had turned his back on his entire life in France.

Of course she had the address of the village in Kabylia. But all her letters remained unanswered.

Annie's emotional life was on ice: all she could do was work, and gain promotion at the office. Then, two years later, a letter arrived at the Anjou village. It was addressed to Annie's father—the two men had got along fairly well. But the envelope contained so little: a photograph of Fatima, a little girl of almost three, tall, thin and dark-haired, posing among her boy and girl cousins. She was standing, while the others were sitting all around her, like a Princess's entourage. On the back of the picture was written, in a laborious hand, the words: 'Fatima is well. Is happy.'

Idir did not sign his name. But he got into the habit of sending, every year on Fatima's birthday, another photograph, though sometimes these turned out to be blurred or of poor quality. Each time there was a fresh snippet of news—'Fatima is going to school'—and still no signature. The packages were always addressed to the grandfather in Anjou. 'As if Fatima's picture could only travel between these two men!' sighed Annie.

In the years that followed, she noticed without commenting that her daughter was now standing in the midst of younger children, three, then four: her brothers and sisters, of course.

Finally she decided to take advantage of a new Franco-Algerian legal protocol and obtained permission to visit.

What was it that finally made her shake off the helpless paralysis which had afflicted her for so long? My sister, her friend throughout these years, explained it to me over the telephone:

'You see,' she said, 'when Annie told me she was learning Berber so that one day she'd be able to talk to her daughter, it struck me. You know we always talk about relearning the lost "mother tongue"—and for me that's what Berber is. I want to speak it like my grandmother, because my mother rejected it! But Annie, you see, wants to discover "her daughter's tongue".'

She wanted, in other words, to learn a language which was not a question of her roots, but of her future. I could see how this would have made everything inside her spring back into action.

When Annie returned to Algiers a few days later, she told me what had happened. She had arrived in Constantine, and from there she took a coach to a little neighbouring town, and went to the office of the lawyer who was expecting her. She slept at the town's only hotel, where a room had been booked for her.

In the morning, at the attorney's office, Idir's brother arrived, a young man with an open expression and a polite manner. He told her, in impeccable French, that her ex-husband refused to see her, as she had come 'through official channels'.

He left, and returned one hour later. This time he was accompanied by a girl. She looked older than ten. The two men went out, leaving Annie and Fatima in a sort of visitor's room.

There was silence between them. Annie's eyes were wide, her face remained impassive, and her hands extended in a tentative gesture, not even a caress. Fatima stared at her, the little girl's face long and delicate, her features as if drawn with a brush, and that fiery gaze slowly taking in the stranger.

Fatima spoke first. In, surprise, surprise, a French definitely learned at school, borrowed:

'What's your name?'

'Annie.'

'Annie,' repeated Fatima. She then told Annie her own name, pronouncing it not exactly as it had lived for so long in the visitor's heart: the i was not a French i, but something between an é and an i. Annie would learn that pronunciation later, and get it right.

Fatima continued, hesitantly, or rather sceptically:

'My father (she said those two words proudly and Annie was pleased), my father doesn't know that I know. I've been told.'

'What have you been told?' murmured Annie with a tremor in her voice. She thought how she had prepared, in the crude little hotel, a long sentence of love in Berber for her daughter. How could she say it, get it out, confess? The little girl wanted to reply, her curiosity seemed to be aroused, but she was holding back:

'What have you been told?' Annie's hands reached out to Fatima's shoulder. The girl did not flinch. She did not recoil.

'The children at school—the boys say I've got a French mother.' Suddenly, in a clear, incisive tone: 'Are you the French woman?'

The child did not move: her features were motionless, the brown of her forehead almost bistre, her eyes slightly dark around the edges; she wore a vague expression, feigned indifference or coldness—and Annie, numb, felt herself go weak inside. She said nothing. She contemplated her daughter. Her little girl; no longer so little.

'Dare I hug her?' she wondered, 'Me, the French woman!' She stretched out her hand, her fingers, wanting to brush Fatima's cheek. Who did not move. She simply stared fixedly.

Suddenly, Annie said, she took the plunge and spoke at length. A very, very, long sentence, just for Fatima, her daughter, the little girl who had grown up alone and who held herself upright, with that impassive older-woman look wielded like a sword before her. Annie poured out everything in one sentence, her love, her pain, the fact that she only had one little girl, that she would never have any other children . . .

She probably lost herself in these over-passionate words. Fatima must have suffered it as an avalanche, a torrent, a hail of little stones. There were no caresses, no; or not yet. Annie stopped her story, and then said to me, in a different voice:

'It's true, it was suddenly as if I had another voice, as if another person was inside me, a stranger who was somehow still me, or a dead woman from the past brought to life again through me. And this other voice inside me—the voice of a lost little girl—recited the Berber sentence I had learned the previous evening. Written at the hotel, in the Roman alphabet and then in Tifinagh: my little sentence of love!'

Annie got her breath back, then admitted:

'Fatima stared at me, she smiled slowly, almost mysteriously, like . . . ' She cast around for the right words: 'like an Italian painting of a Madonna.'

I held my tongue. I was getting ready to take her to the

airport. She was going back to France.

Annie went on, immersed in the memory:

'It was wonderful! But it was also . . . Oh Isma . . . ' she said to me, 'it was so hard! I haven't told you yet: Fatima, who to my surprise spoke French and Arabic, and Berber of course, Fatima at the age of nine and a half wears a black chador which comes down to her shoulders. I wanted her to show me her hair, I wanted her to take off that scarf. Oh, not straight away: but I plucked up the courage to ask her when I sensed that it would soon be time for us to part. It's silly, but I so wanted to see her hair. Silky or curly, black or auburn, it didn't matter! Just to see it. And yet she refused my request, and it was a deliberate refusal that truly came from her.'

I could see Annie going over it in her mind, her face drawn from fatigue or pain. 'During our conversation,' she said, 'one thing shocked me above all. Fatima had spoken to me about the fast that was ending and how she had just fasted—at such a young age! She said she had got used to the idea of having a French mother, but not a mother who did not observe the Muslim fast. I tried to explain about the many different religions, and even that people can be "outside religion". She gave me the same cold look that she had given me at first. That is why, I know, she didn't want to take off her chador for me.'

We left for the airport. In the car, Annie began counting the months until summer. She grew more confident, blossomed: she would come, next summer, and spend a whole month near Annaba. The two of them would get to know each other better; they would love each other: Annie and Fatima.

And, as she kissed me, Annie gave me a letter to post: 'My Berber sentence in the two alphabets that I should have given to her. Do you think, Isma, that her father will come between us?'

I did not have the time to reassure her. Another minute and she would have missed the plane.

I waved goodbye, her letter in my hand like a pennant.   □

Translation by Ros Schwartz

GRANTA

DAVID MACEY
FORT-DE-FRANCE

Frantz Fanon

Outside, the sun is still hot. In an hour or so, the bats will fly during a brief twilight. And then the tree frogs will begin to chirp in the dark. The temperature will not fall significantly. Inside the bar, air-conditioning ensures that it is pleasantly cool, and the drinks are cold. There is no terrace, and there are no tables on the pavement: depending on the season, it is either too hot or too wet to drink outside. It isn't crowded. The Americans have gone back to the cruise ships for their fourth meal of the day, leaving local restaurateurs to grumble that they eat so much aboard that they have no appetite to eat anything on shore. On an island where tourism is promoted as the miracle product that will at last ensure economic growth, they prefer their visitors hungry.

The whites in the bar are speaking French, but the black customers and staff are not. According to all the guidebooks they should be speaking an exotically cooing language; instead, they are speaking something harsh and guttural, at a speed that defies understanding. It is Creole, a rich gumbo of French, African survivals and remnants of all the European languages that have ever been spoken on the island by sailors, traders and slavers. The wall-mounted television in the corner is showing Rowan Atkinson in *The Thin Blue Line*, rather badly dubbed into French. No one seems to be watching: funny British coppers are incomprehensible here. Then comes a news broadcast, a report on the strike at a Renault car plant in Belgium, which is almost 4,000 miles away. It is in French, and is being retransmitted from a studio in Paris. Similarly, the tropical fruit drink I am sipping was canned in France and then flown or shipped across the Atlantic to an island where mangoes and pineapples will grow without human encouragement. This is Martinique. Martinique is in France and its capital, as local people say with a bitter smile, is Paris.

My confusion as to where I am has been growing all day. Or rather, it began yesterday, at Charles de Gaulle airport in Paris. Flights for Martinique depart from the long-haul international terminal, but passengers can buy only a limited range of goods from the duty-free shops—and the range does not include spirits. Passengers for Martinique do not cross any national borders and therefore enjoy no concessions. After eight hours in the air, I am still in the European Union, still in a familiar France. And also in a very unfamiliar France. On the way from the airport to Fort-de-France—the true capital of Martinique—my taxi passed the same sprawl of supermarkets, furniture warehouses and DIY stores that clutters the approaches to so many French towns, but only after driving along a motorway with a banana plantation on the right and fields of sugar cane on the left. The streets of Fort-de-France have familiar names—rue Schoelcher, rue Victor Hugo, rue Lamartine, rue Anatole France, boulevard du Général de Gaulle—and tell a familiar (French) story. But there is a different story to be told about Martinique, one that is not quite French.

To wander through these streets is to experience both familiarity and a profound sense of strangeness. Shoehorned into the plain (once a marsh) that lies between two sluggish rivers and forms an amphitheatre between steep hills and the sea, the centre of Fort-de-France is so small, and the grid of narrow streets so regular, that it is impossible to become lost. It is also impossible not to feel lost. Fort-de-France is in many ways a reproduction of the provincial French town, but the reproduction is flawed. The gleaming white public buildings—the town hall, the courthouse, the police headquarters, the central post office—could have been airlifted in, but they stand on streets pitted with potholes where old ladies sit under parasols and try to sell a handful of fruit or a few fish. The astonishing tropical vegetation insists that this is not France. Breadfruit, mangoes and traveller's trees do not grow in Normandy. High in the green hills to the north, I can see a building that provokes a shock of recognition, and then a sense of bewilderment. It is a small-scale replica of Montmartre's Sacré-Coeur, built here in honour of the Martinican soldiers who died for France in the First World War. It is also a monument to the attempt to recreate France in the Caribbean. In Montmartre, the white church is surrounded by plane trees and looks out over a grey city; this tropical Sacré-Coeur is set among palms and overlooked by conical peaks clad with dense vegetation.

Martinique has been French since the seventeenth century, but it has not always been part of France. Until 1946, it was a colony with a governor, but it then became a *département* like any other and acquired the same constitutional status as Loir-et-Cher or the Pas-de-Calais. Martinique is one of four overseas *départements* and, like Guadeloupe, Réunion and Guyane, it is a fragment of the old empire that was lost to Britain in the eighteenth century when France retained its sugar islands and surrendered Canada (famously dismissed by Voltaire as a 'few acres of snow'). Guadeloupe and Martinique are in the Lesser Antilles, Réunion in the Indian Ocean, and Guyane (formerly French Guyana) is part of the Latin American land mass. Their inhabitants are full French citizens, but the four overseas *départements* rarely impinge upon the awareness of metropolitan France, except when it is time to book an exotic holiday. It comes as quite a shock to stand on a hot, palm-fringed beach in Martinique and realize that soon, if all goes according to plan, this island will be part of the European Monetary Union.

Martinique's new status was not simply foisted upon it in 1946. The people of the island voted in favour of its assimilation into France. For the black majority, this offered protection against the minority of white *békés*, who are descended from the first white plantation owners to be born in Martinique. The etymology of the word is uncertain, but it is said to derive from an Ibo word meaning both 'white' and 'foreigner'. As an ethno-class, the *békés* were not unsympathetic to greater autonomy from the France that had permitted, or even encouraged, the rise of a black middle class with considerable political power. Departmentalization also guaranteed some protection against American influence. Independence or decolonization was not on offer, and the appalling example of Haiti was there to show what it might lead to if it were. Voluntary assimilation seemed a positive alternative to continued colonization.

Under the old colonial system, Martinique supplied France with agricultural produce and imported manufactured goods in return. The small-scale production of cotton, coffee and indigo was not successful, but sugar became the answer to the colony's problems. It inspired the development of a plantation economy which required slaves from Africa, since the Caribs who exterminated the aboriginal population of Amerindians had been exterminated in their turn by the first colonists. All black Martinicans are descended from slaves, and it is virtually impossible to trace their ancestry beyond 1848, when slavery was finally abolished. Before that date, family records disappear into the anonymity of a slave system in which there was no place for individuals with names and ancestries of their own. According to their own tradition, the *békés* could trace a supposedly pure bloodline back to France, but blacks take great pleasure in pointing out that it is more likely to go back to the slums of the Atlantic ports than to a chateau on the Loire. And a stroll through the streets of Fort-de-France will convince anyone that, in Martinique, pure bloodlines are very rare. It is obvious that its people are of mixed descent: they derive from black Africans, the indentured Indians who replaced slaves in the cane fields, Chinese and Syrian merchants, and white planters.

Sugar is still produced, but the industry has been in decline for most of this century. Cane grown on mountain plantations and cut by hand cannot compete with sugar beet grown on the plains of northern France and harvested mechanically. Martinique's bananas are delicious, but they are small and irregular-shaped, and compete badly with the designer fruit produced by American-owned multinationals on vast plantations in Latin America. The advertisements on the buses that urge Parisians to consume 'home-grown' bananas from Martinique and Guadeloupe appear to have little impact. The island *département* has no real economy and seems to exist in a financial limbo. Unemployment is high, but so too are French social security payments and family allowances. The inflated state sector is a major employer, and civil servants' salaries are forty per cent higher than they would be in France. Property prices are high. Poverty certainly exists, but in general the standard of living, health care and education is higher than in the other Caribbean islands. Virtually all consumer goods are imported from France. The streets are choked with imported cars. There is a good local beer, but it has to compete with brews from Alsace. Even 'tropical' produce can have a strange provenance: supermarkets sell yams that were grown in central France. Other imports are from further afield. The pretty shell bracelets in the craft market were made in the Philippines or Indonesia; the T-shirts are made from Egyptian cotton and were printed in Europe. I eventually bought wooden toy machetes for my children. The pokerwork letters on the blades spell 'Martinique', but the handles are stamped 'Made in Haiti'.

The central market that was once the belly of Fort-de-France now specializes in selling overpriced gift packets of spices to tourists who could buy them much more cheaply in Paris. The women selling fruit and vegetables, the scrawny chickens tethered by the leg and the stalls selling cordials and mysterious bottles whose contents have magical rather than medicinal properties, function as an exotic backdrop to the real business of tourism. A local economy has been elbowed aside. The market is a female preserve, and some of the women traders wear the traditional costume of a checked cotton skirt, an off-the-shoulder white blouse and a headscarf twisted into a turban. *Adieu madras, adieu foulard* . . . the madras skirt and the headscarf are the traditional trappings of nostalgic songs about doomed love affairs between the black girl and the white officer with a wife and children in France. In the stories and songs, he always leaves her once he has consumed her like some piece of exotic fruit. She was his *doudou*, his love or his darling, and the image of the beautiful 'native girl' (who is of course also a native of France) now adorns the posters and postcards that sell the promise of tropical sex. A Martinican can still use *'ma doudou'* as an affectionate form of address; but for the tourist, a *doudou* is a tacky statuette of a caricatural black woman to be bought in a souvenir shop. Traditional costume is now worn only by those involved, however peripherally, in the tourist industry. Tourists complain when these women refuse to be photographed without being paid. A white Frenchman attempting to photograph a particularly elusive hummingbird in an exotic garden jokingly grumbles that even the birds want to be paid here, just like the people. A white woman sneaks a photograph of the beautiful black baby in its mother's arms, and then thanks the woman, who did not know her child's image was being collected for someone's holiday album. Tourists staying in four-star hotels do not want to buy fish from the market, but they do want to photograph the old woman selling the fish. White France turns black France into a souvenir.

White France is everywhere on this black island. The little girl on her way to school is carrying a paperback edition of

Perrault's tales, as her equivalent in France might do. What will she make of the tale of Little Red Riding Hood? There are no wolves here, and never have been. Her book does not tell Martinique's own folk tales about zombies, three-legged horses and shape-shifters who can take off their human skins, hang them up and then fly off into the night. Her reading is in keeping with the rest of her education. Living on an island where the year is divided into wet and dry seasons, she will have been taught that there are four seasons and that it snows at Christmas. She will have been discouraged from speaking the Creole that is in effect her first language. Unless an enthusiastic teacher offers an option in 'local history', her history classes will not be about Martinique, but about revolutions and republics founded and overthrown in Paris. And that, on the whole, is the history told by the streets of Fort-de-France. It is a very specific history; most of the figures who have given their names to streets are associated with secular republicanism, none more so than Victor Schoelcher, the architect of the abolition of slavery whose statue stands outside the courthouse. The kindly paternalist is showing a black child the road to freedom. The girl is on her way to school, where she will be taught that the France of the Rights of Man and the Citizen abolished slavery. Another statue in Fort-de-France hints, despite itself, that something about this story is not quite right. It is of Josephine de Beauharnais, wife to Napoleon Bonaparte, Empress of the French, and daughter of Martinique. For some, she is still an object of devotion; for others she is the woman who influenced Napoleon's decision to reintroduce the slavery that had been technically abolished in 1793. A few years ago, someone removed her head and it has never been replaced. The headless statue of a woman in an Empire dress of cotton is daubed with red paint, and the pedestal bears a crude inscription in Creole: *Respet ba Matnik*: 'Respect for Martinique'.

Thirty-two kilometres south of Fort-de-France, the streets of the little town of Rivière-Pilote also tell a story. This is the stronghold of a small pro-independence party: a plaque in the rue des Insurrections anti-esclavagistes records the history of the slave rebellions that began almost as soon as slavery was introduced.

The first occurred in 1639, only four years after Martinique was seized by France. The last occurred in 1848, and forced the Governor to declare that slavery had been abolished before the official proclamation arrived from Paris. The last words on the orange plaque are in Creole and read: *Nég pété chenn*: 'the black man broke his chains'. This is a very rare example of Creole being used for official purposes. There is no mention of Victor Schoelcher. The neighbouring rue du Marronage commemorates the runaway slaves, or *marrons,* who fled into the hills and occasionally raided the plantations of the hated *békés*. Those who beheaded Josephine have their ancestors.

In June 1997, the people of Rivière-Pilote elected a pro-independence *député* to represent them in Paris. Here, one has a sense of stepping into a Martinique which has its own history, its own language and its own culture—one which France cannot quite assimilate. And it is quite easy, here, to walk away from French Martinique: you only have to go to the library. The history books tell the official story, but writers such as Edouard Glissant, Patrick Chamoiseau and Raphaël Confiant tell the tales that lie beneath and beyond it. Chamoiseau's *Texaco* describes the inexorable growth of a shanty town that spread like some urban mangrove swamp on the outskirts of Fort-de-France; Confiant's *Le Nègre et l'Amiral* is a chronicle of the Second World War in Martinique, written in a style imitating that of the traditional storytellers who wove fantastic tales around fires in village huts; Glissant's novels and poems record Creole history.

You can leave France behind, too, on the Pointe-du-bout promontory, across the bay from Fort-de-France. The seafront has been concreted over with a hotel complex that would not be out of place on the Côte d'Azur—it makes no concessions to the local architectural tradition. But only a few hundred metres away from it you can watch a man with a machete at his side manipulating a curious wooden box with a hinged lid. He is setting a trap for land crabs. Stuffed land crabs are a local delicacy, and taste particularly good when accompanied by punch. In many restaurants customers are given a glass of ice cubes with a slice of lime, a bottle of rum and a bottle of cane-*sirop*, and left to mix their own (some visitors find this offhand service disconcerting, even insulting; others worry that the descendants of slaves might not enjoy being treated like servants). Or you can leave the marina at Le Marin on the south coast—worthy of Cannes, and clearly not intended for local fishing boats—and find streets of wooden houses where chickens are kept in backyards. I went to one café where the menu featured curried goat and breadfruit washed down with local beer, rather than the steak-and-chips-and-red-wine on offer on the expensive waterfront. The bird-feeder hanging by the door contained sugared water for the hummingbirds that glinted in the sunlight. A fortnight in Martinique does not have to be just another fortnight in France.

Somewhere in the statistics collected by the Martinique Tourist Board in 1997, there will be a record of the response given by a white Englishman who, on being asked his main reason for visiting the island, said simply: 'Frantz Fanon' and then added, 'I'm writing his biography.' This must have put me in a statistical category of my own. English visitors to Martinique are rare: most tourists come from France, and come for sun and sea, not for information about the once-celebrated author of *Black Skin, White Masks* and *The Wretched of the Earth*—two violently eloquent calls to arms which inspired self-styled revolutionaries across the world, and made Fanon someone to be discussed in the same breath as Ho Chi Minh and Che Guevara. My old copies of these books are inscribed PARIS, 1970. I bought them at a time when it was still possible to believe that a Third World revolution could provoke radical change in the West. As the Black Power leader Stokely Carmichael put it: 'Every brother on a rooftop can quote Fanon.' Back then, we all wanted to join the brothers.

But the young woman I spoke to on a black volcanic beach on the Caribbean coast was more intrigued by my nationality than by my interest in a long-dead author. Perhaps it was an inappropriate place to be discussing him. This beach had other echoes. It lay below the volcano which on the morning of 8 August 1902 erupted and destroyed the town of St Pierre. Thirty thousand people died in ten minutes; the sea boiled as ships laden with rum and sugar caught fire. It wasn't a Fanon shrine: instead, it was a place to watch the frigate birds drifting over the sea, and the fisherman hauling ashore a seine-net with the help of some tourists who had the right to a share of the fish as their reward.

Frantz Fanon was born in 1925 and brought up in Martinique's black-mulatto community. Like all Martinicans, he was taught that he was French, and that he belonged to a universal republic. The black boy was taught to put on a white mask, to speak French and not Creole. Creole was the language of the plantations and was not spoken by the respectable children of customs officers; French was a step up an evolutionary ladder, and France cheerfully described its successfully assimilated colonial subjects as *évolués*: they had evolved beyond native status and were on their way to becoming truly French. The young Fanon did not know that *évolué* could also be used in the derogatory sense of 'uppity'.

Of course he realized that he was black, or at least a 'man of colour'. But he did not know that he was a *nègre* (which, depending on the context and the speaker's politics, can mean both 'negro' and 'nigger'). So far as people in the Martinique of the 1920s and 1930s were concerned, *nègres* lived in Africa and were inferior to Martinicans; many an educated Martinican had served as an administrator in France's African colonies, and had *nègres* under his direct orders. The young Fanon also knew where *nègres* came from. He had seen them in 'Tarzan' films, and identified not with them but with the white lord of the jungle. And he had seen *tirailleurs sénégalais* in transit in Fort-de-France. *They* were *nègres*: black colonial troops recruited in Africa who enjoyed a formidable reputation for rape and looting (practices actively encouraged by their white officers), as well as for courage in battle. Advertising tamed that fearsome reputation. The image of a grinning *tirailleur sénégalais* in his distinctive red cap was used from 1917 onwards to sell Banania, a breakfast food made from banana flour and cocoa. The caption read *'Y'a bon, Banania'*, a copywriter's caricatural perception of how an African says: *'Banania, c'est bon'* ('Banania is good').

In 1943 the eighteen-year-old Fanon left Martinique as a volunteer in an infantry unit, convinced that France's war was his war. (The *békés* thought otherwise: none of them volunteered. From 1940 to 1943, they had supported a local version of the

Vichy regime and had replaced elected black mayors with white appointees.) By late 1944, Fanon was disillusioned and feeling betrayed by the racial absurdities of French military life. He wrote to his parents that he had been 'mistaken' when he volunteered. He was fighting alongside some *tirailleurs sénégalais* in France, but the *nègres* wore the distinctive uniform that marked them as 'not included', while Fanon, as a citizen from an old colony, fought in French uniform. It was his new white mask.

In Europe, 8 May marks the anniversary of the end of a war. On the other side of the Mediterranean, it is remembered for more sinister reasons. Victory celebrations in three small towns in the French *département* of the Constantinois in eastern Algeria turned into pro-independence demonstrations, and home-made Algerian flags were flown. The police opened fire. Accurate statistics are impossible to come by, but the official Algerian estimate is that 15,000 died in the repression that followed. Many a 'French' soldier returning from the battlefields of Europe went home to learn that a relative had been killed by French bullets. One of them was Ahmed Ben Bella, who was to become the first President of independent Algeria. A new war had begun, and it would not end until 1962.

Fanon was probably not the only French soldier to find it odd that the once-colonized were liberating their colonizers. It was white France that taught Fanon he was a *nègre*, and that the grinning face on the Banania poster was his. In metropolitan France, he could be mistaken for an Arab and taken in for questioning by the police. The mask was slipping, and France would not recognize what lay beneath it. White France, for Fanon, took the form of the girls who would not dance with him and his comrades in the towns they liberated. It took the form of the peasant farmers of the Doubs who seemed to have no interest in their own liberation, and showed no gratitude towards a black Frenchman who had risked his life for them. After the war, it took the form of the lecturer who addressed Fanon with a demeaningly familiar *tu* during an oral examination in Lyon (guidebooks still have to warn metropolitan tourists not to be too free with *tu* when they visit Martinique). The lecturer was addressing a decorated and wounded war veteran who was completing a degree in medicine, but spoke to him as though he were a child, or a *nègre*. When he first treated Arab patients, Fanon found to his horror that he himself fell into the white doctor's role and addressed them as *tu*. White France, by this time, was the child who saw Fanon and turned to its mother with the words: 'Look, a *nègre* . . . Mummy, I'm frightened.'

Fanon remained in France when the war ended, and trained as a doctor in Lyon. He specialized in psychiatry and in 1953, after serving a clinical apprenticeship in metropolitan hospitals, was appointed to a post at the modern psychiatric hospital in Blida, a suburb of Algiers. Algeria had been relatively quiet since 1945, but a few terrorist incidents had signalled what was to come; and the bombs that went off in November 1954 made it even clearer. But for France, there never was a 'war' in Algeria; Algeria was part of a greater France—the Mediterranean ran through it, just as the Seine runs through Paris. And a nation-state could not declare war on its own territory. So France could use its army only to conduct police operations and to control 'the events in Algeria'. For the nationalists of the Front de Libération National, these 'events' were both a war of independence and a revolution.

In Blida, Fanon tried to reform a colonial psychiatry that categorized all Algerians as potential criminals governed by murderously violent impulses, and to argue that the symptoms his patients presented had to be studied and treated in terms of a cultural system that was not French. There was little point, he thought, in setting tests featuring crosses in a cemetery for patients living in a land where there are no crosses in cemeteries. It struck him that the very idea of psychiatry was absurd in a country where doctors revived the victims of torture only to allow them to be tortured again. In any case, his sympathies lay with those he called 'the wretched of the earth', the landless peasants and the dispossessed who had crowded into the slums of Algiers. He resigned, was expelled from Algeria and went into exile in Tunis, where he worked as a journalist, a propagandist, and a roving ambassador for the self-declared Provisional Government of the Republic of Algeria. Fanon had found his war. He did not survive it, though he escaped more than one assassination attempt. Eight months before Algerian independence, Fanon died of leukaemia.

In *The Wretched of the Earth*, his last book, he spoke with a new voice: 'We Algerians . . . ' France had not given him that identity; its acquisition was an act of political will. And yet it was not, of course, a stable identity. Just as there are still those in Martinique who regard him as a traitor who betrayed the France that had educated him, so there are Algerians who refuse to recognize him as a brother, on the grounds that a black non-Muslim cannot be a full member of an Arab-Islamic nation. That is why it is so difficult to reconcile Fanon's story with the official history of Martinique, which insists that a European nation-state really can transcend its geographical boundaries to include islands in the Caribbean and the Indian Ocean. France proposes itself as a nation that can ignore ethnic differences and colour and create citizens who are neither black nor white, but French, and therefore heirs to a universal civilization. Those citizens naturally speak French and not Creole (or, some might add, Breton or Basque). Quite simply, France still imagines that it includes Martinique, just as it once included Algeria. Fanon's story exposes the cracks in this whole idea of France's inclusive unity.

Fanon's reliability as a guide to modern Martinique is dubious. He ignores the beauty of the island, and uses metaphors of illness and decay to describe a Fort-de-France which looks shabby, but not disease-ridden. It is no longer the backward colony he loathed. The rise of a black middle class and the decline of the old plantation system makes the black–white divide less obvious, if only because the small white population is so invisible in Fort-de-France, though it still clings to economic power and controls the main local bank. Young people still gather on the Savanne, the grassy square in Fort-de-France where Fanon once played football under Josephine's stony gaze. Football is still played there on Sunday mornings, but after dark the Savanne is home to drug-users and drunks carrying bottles of cheap white rum. And yet the sense of cultural alienation described by *Black Skin, White Masks* is palpable even to a white tourist. This is, for instance, a place where cigarettes and rum are cheaper than in metropolitan France, and books and newspapers more expensive.

Fanon describes French dominance as inducing a psychosis centred on the need to 'whiten' Martinique and as creating a climate in which black people liked neither themselves nor each other; a recent sociological study shows that adolescent girls still dream of marrying white husbands. Divisions between blacks, mulattos and Indians (confusingly described as 'coolies') still exist, and the language of shadism is such an everyday reality that this is no place for the politically correct. A *câpresse* is a woman with long wavy hair and a cinnamon skin. A *chabin* is a man with blue eyes, reddish hair and a lightish skin, who is the distant descendant of a *béké* and a black woman. A novelist like Patrick Chamoiseau can admit with a sad smile that Martinicans are still ill at ease with their black skins (and, no doubt, with my white skin, though he is too polite to say so).

Fanon's name is faintly inscribed on the fabric of Fort-de-France: there is an Avenue Frantz Fanon and a Frantz Fanon Arts Centre. But it does not really feel at home here and is at odds with the other names on public display. It feels more comfortable in Rivière-Pilote, where the Frantz Fanon Library houses a good collection of his works. It seems appropriate that the library should stand in a town which officially remembers slave rebellions and runaways rather than French poets and politicians. Like the *béké* on horseback with a whip in his hand, the runaway slave in the forest is a figure that haunts Martinique's imagination, and part of the image's power derives from the fact that there were so few *marrons*: there are not many places to run to on an island with a surface area of 1,000 square kilometres, and where it is easy to feel that the sea is a prison wall. The story of Frantz Fanon, indeed, is such a rare one that it is tempting to see him as a latter-day *marron*, perpetually trying to flee a France that wanted forcibly to include him.

I am sitting in a café in Paris, killing time before I go to the airport for the evening flight home to England. I often come to Paris to work in libraries and archives, and to talk to Fanon's surviving friends and relations. There is, or should be, research to be done in Algeria too, but I can't go there: there's another war going on. This time it is between Islamic 'fundamentalists' and a

73

repressive government. No one knows how many people have died: 80,000, 100,000? But I do know that I might not make it alive from the airport to the centre of Algiers.

But here in Paris, one of Algeria's daughters is walking down the street outside. She is in her teens and is wearing a long skirt. She is also wearing a *hijab*, or a headscarf which conceals her hair and throat, leaving only the oval of her face visible. Her headscarf or foulard is drab. She is clearly on her way to school, but will she be allowed to attend? Since the early 1990s, girls dressed like this have regularly been excluded for refusing to take off their headscarves. French schools are militantly secular, and the day does not begin with an act of collective worship, Christian or otherwise. Pupils are forbidden by law from wearing conspicuous religious insignia, though the legislators have omitted to supply any definition of 'conspicuous' (I have never heard of a Christian being excluded from school for wearing a cross around his or her neck). The legal debate over the contradiction between secularism in schools and the constitutional guarantee of religious freedom goes on. Occasionally, it is pointed out by an academic or journalist that secularism was originally designed to protect Jews and Protestants from a Catholic majority that was hostile to godless republicanism, but that it is now being invoked to exclude Muslims. More problematic still, a disastrous confusion between race and religion is growing. Schools have interpreted the wearing of a *hijab* as an unequivocal statement of belief: 'I am a Muslim.' Sections of the press have even construed it as a gesture of support for fundamentalism. Hence the exclusion of certain girls from the very institutions that are supposed to make them French.

A girl wearing a *hijab* is clearly making a statement, but it may be an ambiguous one. It can be a statement of religious belief, or a statement of ethnic pride. It can also be a way of negotiating a compromise: a way for young women to walk down the street without being chaperoned by their brothers. The association of the headscarf with fundamentalism, and hence with terrorism, is almost automatic, but it is a misperception of a complex symbol. Ironically, there are parts of Algiers where it would be dangerous to go out wearing only a *hijab*, and not the *haik* that conceals the entire face. The result could be rape, or even murder.

In the end Fanon found it impossible to be a black Frenchman, impossible to go on wearing a white mask. He became Algerian, lived, fought and died as an Algerian. In the opinion of Edouard Glissant, this is why he is so uncomfortable a figure for many of his fellow Martinicans. Of all the black francophone intellectuals, he was the only one whose commitment took him so far. *Nég pété chenn*. The slave took to the hills. His flight was an individual one, and one for exceptional times. He probably does not provide a model for the young blacks of the suburbs, who know that they are not *nègres*, whatever anyone else may say. Increasingly, they regard themselves as *black*, and use the Anglo-American term to defy white France and turn an imposed marginality into a positive identity, just as some young North Africans refuse to be defined as either French or Arab, and call themselves *beurs*, a word derived from a slang term for 'Arab'. They have no need for white masks. The appeal of rap and *rai*, a swirling blend of Arab and European rhythms originating from western Algeria (and deemed unIslamic by the fundamentalists; many musicians have been forced by death threats to seek refuge in France and some have been killed), is such that some white youths would probably like to don black masks. *The Wretched of the Earth*'s messianic prophecies of a violent Third World revolution that will sweep away colonialism now look false, and the fundamentalists of the Islamic Salvation Front have adapted Fanon's words on the necessity of violence to ends he could never have accepted.

But while Fanon may not provide a model, his *Black Skin, White Masks* does help to reveal some of the fault lines that make a certain idea of France more uncertain than ever. Reading it makes it difficult to accept at face value a certain self-image cultivated by France. Like any nation, France is what has been termed an imagined community. What it imagines itself to be determines what it can remember and what it must forget. The abolition of slavery can be remembered, but not the 200 years of suffering that preceded it. The French and Martinican soldiers who died in Algeria must be remembered, but not the Algerian civilians who died on the streets of Paris when the police opened fire on a demonstration called in 1961 to protest at the curfew imposed on the Algerian community. It is hard for France to remember Fanon, but nor is he easily remembered in either Algeria or Martinique. A survey of French psychology students in Paris found that, while most had heard of Fanon, few knew that he was a psychiatrist; Algerian school students who know that he worked with the FLN do not always know that he was black.

In Martinique, France tries to include. At home, it often excludes. Inside the frontier that crosses the Atlantic, lines of exclusion can be drawn across school gates. Every summer, the press tells the story of the black or North African youth group from one of Paris's dreary suburbs that went camping by the sea. They had a firm booking on a campsite, but when they got there the site was full and, no, there was no record of a reservation. No campsite in France operates a discriminatory policy, it's just that someone has made a mistake. The story will be told again next summer. France imagines that its frontiers can ignore the Atlantic, and forgets that they include a not-quite-France that it cannot quite comprehend.

Strange things happen to statues in Martinique. The war memorial in the little town of Le Lorrain features a statue of a soldier in First World War uniform. His face was once black, but now it has been painted bright pink. If Le Lorrain is in France, and not in a not-quite-France, surely his black skin has its place in her memory. In Martinique, France draws a line which excludes a whole history just as, at home, it can draw invisible lines around campsites and schools. France forgets that its borders for a long time included Algeria, which it now tries to exclude because it cannot imagine it as anything other than a threat. It imagines that its own culture is universal, and therefore does not need to acknowledge plural cultures. The icon of the Republic is a woman—Marianne—whose statue is displayed in every town hall. But there are no statues of a black Marianne, and a girl in a *hijab* in Paris can be barred from the very institution that is supposed to make her French. In Martinique, meanwhile, the children are still taught that it will snow at Christmas. □

GRANTA

PATRICK CHAMOISEAU
THE RAT

Fort-de-France, at that time, had not yet declared war on rats. Along with the crabs, they inhabited the crumbled sidewalks and canals of the city. They haunted the gullies. They scoured the basements; they emerged in the nocturnal refuse and accompanied the insomniac strolls of lunar poets. A colony of them padded about in the staircase of the house. Absorbed with his spiders, his cockroaches and his dragonflies, the little boy didn't notice them right away. A few squeaks here and there. A fleeting shadow in the canal. But during one of his moments of stillness on the roof of the kitchens, he came upon a fabulous spectacle. Here's how.

At about one in the afternoon, Fort-de-France became lethargic, with fewer pedestrians and fewer horns. Country people sought refuge in the shade to eat. The Syrians lowered the iron curtains of their shops. The dust of this urban desert began to flutter. Behind the house, on the roof of the kitchens, a shadow offered a cool haven for the little boy. On Saturday afternoons, the languor deepened. Families went off to the country, to mass, to a catechism or to take care of other business. Finally, the house creaked under the weight of silence, and the little boy was free to do nothing, to be still. It was on a day like this when a squeak lifted him from his inner emptiness, calling him to the edge of the roof. That's when he saw the rats, down in the courtyard. Five or six, yes, there they were—scourers searching for crumbs, tub climbers, tightrope artists on the edge of buckets, disappearing into the kitchens and reappearing just as fast. Very young rats and very old rats. Others, fearful, emerged from the covered canal only to pounce on a titbit of food.

The little boy believed that he was discovering an obscure way of life, which ran parallel to the life of the house. The rats had already—though he didn't know this at the time—caught the attention of the adults. This would only become apparent to him with the arrival of his mother's laying hens, whose eggs the rats carted off with a never-before-seen ingenuity. In the absence of eggs the sharp-toothed little beasts slaughtered chicks by the dozen (and the half-dozen). The massacres were discovered at dawn, before the arrival of the water; the boy heard his mother, Ma Ninotte, shrieking the foulest of morning maledictions. The chicks had been half-devoured and some of the hens had been wounded. The adults put down poison in tiny pink packets, which at first killed the rats in threes and fours, but then became ineffectual. The mousetraps (soaped, sprinkled with disinfectant, scented with fresh meat) attracted no rat if they had already been used. So the campaign lost steam, the diminished colony was forgotten, and, until the next massacre of the chicks, the next early-morning death cry, everyone had to endure the misery of a staircase swarming with invisible rat-life.

The little boy developed a special extermination plan of his own. He would have been perfectly incapable of explaining why; he couldn't have said what provoked this reflex to destroy.

Among the rats there was one that was older than the others: slower, more wary, but powerful and more cunning. He ventured into the open only in conditions of complete security, against a backdrop of pure silence. Not until the floorboards of the house stopped moving, and Fort-de-France shut down and gave in to the dust, did the old rat risk his shadow beneath the vertical heel of the sun. He was massive, and stitched up with scars; he had lost an ear, a piece of his tail, and perhaps also some part of himself which made him no longer merely a rat. He was so experienced it was terrifying: his heart didn't leap at every puff of wind, but his finely tuned ear and acute eye told him when to disappear instantly. He had no habits, never passed the same spot twice and never retreated in the same manner. This was the rat the boy chose as his very first victim.

A strange relationship developed. The boy found a piece of string and created a slip-knot which he laid out in the courtyard. In the middle, he set down a piece of sausage. And with the knot wedged in place, the string in his fist, he sat lookout on the roof.

The idea was to lasso the vicious old rat. But the animal must have disliked sausage—or else the sight of the lasso cast him into a strategic melancholy which kept him in his hole, philosophizing about dark rat affairs. Whatever the case, he never showed up. It was always a younger, stupider rat who ventured into the slip-knot and lunged for the sausage. The boy pulled with all his might—he must have pulled a thousand times. But eventually he had to accept the impossibility of catching a rat with this sausage-lasso set-up. The knot would close around itself, and the impatient boy would haul up nothing but a dangling string.

His next contraption was a basin weighted down by a rock. A piece of wood connected to an invisible string held it in the air. The old rat (he never turned up) was supposed to venture underneath in order to collect the bait. Those who did risk it raced off with the sausage as if conscious of the trap. At other, rarer, times they fled empty-mouthed. After a while, not a single one came. There was the flaming gourd, the infernal jar, the superglue, the rubber band, the guillotine-knife, the poison syrup, the terrifying scissor of doom . . . But even this arsenal of small cruelties was not enough to snare the slightest hint of rat. Too late, he learned that he had to suppress his own smell from the traps, and could never reuse a bait. The rats would avoid any dubious windfalls that lay invitingly within tooth's reach. The boy took some time to understand that, in fact, rats were intelligent.

One day the old rat spotted him. Standing on the edge of the tub, he furtively glanced his way, then pursued his quest. Two inhuman orbs of opaque blackness served as his eyes. For a split second these eyes brushed over him, and, in a certain sense, scorned him. Never again did the old rat, even though he knew the boy was watching, grant him a second glance. He modified his routes and always remained far from the overhang of the roof where the boy—changing his tactics, trying to be selective—was perched, rock in hand, directly above the bait on the ground, waiting to crush the Old Man's back.

Hours of lookout were required, the rock held in his outstretched hand above the void: lying on the tin, watching with only one eye, hoping for silence, breathing in calmness, turning to rust in order to melt into the roof, praying for the old rat to approach, ignoring the other rats that dared to nibble the bait.

Towards the end the boy's stiffened arms would drop the vengeful rock on any frenzied latecomers; but even these avoided being crushed, with leaps that became increasingly leisurely. Their losses beneath the far-too-slow-moving stone never amounted to more than a snippet of tail, a tuft of hair. Around these measly trophies the boy organized pagan ceremonies. The man clutches them today somewhere in his shadows.

The old rat disappeared sometimes, not to be seen for several weeks. The little boy supposed him dead. He imagined secret cemeteries visited by night. He imagined the streets of Fort-de-France covered with all these exhausted rats, who knew their way around poison and who, suddenly hearing some obscure call, would set out to dig a grave with their last tooth. He imagined his ageing adversary, a rat isolated by his years: so much intelligence, such cunning, such caution, so much genius—all ending in dirty dereliction, with no address other than death and forgetting. So the boy arranged funerals for him on tiny cars. A box of matches served as a coffin. The procession travelled the hallway and ended in a liturgy he improvised himself, in rat language. A burial concluded this ceremony—in a hole gouged in the wall near the stairs, where a brick released from its plaster delivered its redness to a burrowing nail. The boy would go away melancholy, missing his old friend, until one day he would see him reappear. Then, rather than rejoicing, he would dash off to invent some atrocity capable of finishing him off, this time for real.

He watched him grow old. It was nothing: a stiffness in the back, a misshapen silhouette, the constant shaking of an ear. He was horrified to see him take risks, react slowly. He caught the Old Man nibbling things he had scoffed at before; and often he seemed immobile, distracted in a senile kind of way. The boy watched him fall apart. A feeling of pity rose up in him: he felt no desire to kill, only the horror of a benign commiseration. He often had the impression that if he came down from the roof, the Old Man would wait for him and allow himself to be touched.

One day, the Old Man limped towards the bait, right under the rock which the boy still brandished, out of habit, from the heights of his lookout. He advanced with a kind of blind—or desperate, or absent-minded—faith, something like a suicidal impulse, or the sense that he had little to lose. He stepped into the trap and began chewing like a church cockroach on the host.

The stone did not crush his skull: it had become the keystone of a cathedral of pity in the child, who wept. □

Translation by CAROL VOLK

Royal Festival Hall
Queen Elizabeth Hall
Purcell Room

Literature Events
on the South Bank

Highlights this autumn include:

Wed 24 Sep **Beryl Bainbridge, Peter Carey and John Fowles**
Fiction International

Tue 30 Sep **Martin Amis, Richard Ford & A.L. Kennedy**
Fiction International

Mon 6 Oct **Gore Vidal**
Sounding the Century
The launch of an unmissable series of lectures
presented in association with BBC Radio 3

Sat 11 Oct **Cautionary Tales**
A new look at Hilaire Belloc's memorable verses with poets
Sophie Hannah and Ian McMillan. Music by Ben Park.
(suitable for children 7 years and upwards)

Tue 4 Nov **Nawal el Saadawi**
Sounding the Century
On the impact of fundamentalism as we move into the 21st century
presented in association with BBC Radio 3

Mon 1 Dec **Camille Paglia**
Sounding the Century
Feminism moving forward
presented in association with BBC Radio 3

Plus... international poetry and fiction from **Andrew Crozier,
Carl Rakosi, Lucien Stryk, Eamonn Sweeney, Les Murray,
Anne Haverty, Paul Durcan** and poets from the **Brazil** and **Peru**

Acacia Avenue: Journeys Through Suburbia
A special series which runs through October and
November featuring Jenny Uglow, Philip Hensher, Jonathan
Meades, Nigel Williams, Michael Bracewell and *Brookside*
creator Phil Redmond

**For tickets and your FREE events
bulletin call 0171 960 4242**

sounding the
century

BBC Radio 3 90-93FM

sbc

CAROLINE LAMARCHE
NIGHT IN THE AFTERNOON

A little entrance hall. A staircase. To the left of the staircase, a door with a window leading into the concierge's room. The door is closed, and there's a note stuck behind the handle: 'I'm at the grocer's. Indicate which room you are using and the time you arrived.' Followed by room numbers from one to ten, with little circles that have to be blacked in. They all have been, except for number seven.

'I'll have a look at the room,' the red-headed man says.

He runs upstairs. I stay where I am, leaning against the front door. And then the door opens, pushing me against the wall, and the concierge comes in. She looks me up and down. She must have been beautiful once, and maybe she still is. I find it hard to judge that kind of tired, rather nonchalant beauty. The red-headed man comes back down.

'I've been up to room seven. Apparently it's the only one free.'

The woman looks at the paper with the circles.

'That's right, number seven. You can have it.'

I thank her and smile, quite boldly. I want her to see that it means nothing for me to come here; it's no different from going somewhere to have a drink or see a show, there's nothing special about this place, it's an ordinary house, and I'm just a weary traveller, a guest being shown to her room for an afternoon nap.

'Two hours,' the woman says. 'Just two hours. Any more and it's extra.'

From what I gather, you pay afterwards. We go upstairs. Our room is on the first floor. There are other doors, all closed. The house is completely silent, as if all these rooms are empty, or as if people really do come here to sleep or to listen in silence to what's happening in the other rooms, what's going to happen in room seven for instance, where the red-headed man is stepping aside now for me to enter.

A big room, a big bed covered with a purple spread, high windows with thick curtains, drawn so tightly that not a speck of sunlight filters into the room, and in a corner, a washbasin and a bidet concealed behind another curtain. I look around, not knowing what to do.

'It's very nice.'

'Do you think so?' he says.

It looks as if he's going to start talking again, so very quickly I say: 'Yes, not bad at all,' and walk around, pretending to be interested in the prints of beautiful naked women in languid poses. But all the while, I'm thinking: he won't be able to stop talking, he'll just grope me half-heartedly and it'll be awful, really awful, I'll have to keep putting him at his ease. I turn back to him and smile encouragingly.

'What now?'

'Get undressed.'

I don't move. I'm expecting him to talk, expecting the same weary litany, the same vague and repetitive words, the same clumsy excuses.

He says nothing.

I turn my back on him and start by taking off my dress. When he sees that I've put on my best set of underwear, in dark red lace as fine and shiny as silk, with a half-cup bra to give extra uplift to the breasts, he won't be able to resist, he'll undress me himself, the way Gilles does, sometimes gently, sometimes feverishly, depending on his mood; his hands will caress me through the material, eager to touch me, moving under my arms, around my breasts, slipping off the straps. But nothing happens. He doesn't say a word. He doesn't compliment me on what I'm wearing. And when at last I'm naked, he still says nothing. I can feel him looking at me, but he doesn't seem the slightest bit aroused; he's looking at me with the eyes of a doctor or a horse dealer, coldly measuring and evaluating, concerned only with surfaces, the texture of the skin, the curve of the back.

'On your knees!'

I kneel by the bed. I used to kneel by my bed to say my prayers when I was a child. Margot used to kneel too, on her swollen knees. She was the one who taught me the words of the prayer. Thank you. Forgive me.

The man grabs the back of my neck, forces my chest down on to the bed and then lets go. Next, he places his hands on my buttocks and starts to knead them the way I used to knead dough for those fruitcakes Margot loved so much. That's how the man takes the measure of my flesh, rapidly, with the flat of his hands, then suddenly he thrusts his fingers into me, like a cook mixing currants or cherries into the dough or hiding a charm in the middle of a cake for Twelfth Night.

'Lie down.'

I get on to the bed and lie on my stomach. 'Spread your legs.' The orders are coming faster now. 'More.'

He grabs my thighs and pulls them wide apart. There's a sound of paper being crumpled angrily, and in the expectant silence of the room the sudden noise fills me with terror. The man slips his hands under me and gropes for my breasts. He kneads them, goes away, returns and places plastic clothes-pegs on them. A sharp pain floods me from my nipples to my armpits. I bite my wrists to stop myself from crying out and raise myself on my elbows, holding my breath. The man pushes me back down on the bed, squashing my chest on to the pegs. My dream of metal brooches with chains and weights, and various jewels puncturing my chest—that dream evaporates. I am the clothes-peg woman.

Again the sound of rustling paper, a noise that drives me crazy. I know what it is now. The man has a bag with him, a bag full of things. He must have been hiding it under his leather jacket. He's taking something else out now. With quick, skilful movements he ties a scarf over my eyes. Then I hear a purring sound, and suddenly the thing is inside me. It doesn't seem especially large, but the man pushes it deep inside, then pulls it out. More paper noises, and there's something else inside me, something bigger this time, that moves and hums. I'm breathing hard, my hands clutching at the sheets, searching desperately for something to hold on to. The thing comes out, more rustling of paper, then the man is on top of me, holding my wrists together and twisting a rope three times around them and pulling it very tight, all with the same rapid and precise movements. I can feel something new at the entrance to my vagina, something that doesn't move or make a noise, he rams it in brutally and it dilates me, I feel as if I'm going to explode, this thing is swelling inside me, it's stiff and yet flexible, he pushes it in deeper, I lift my chest in panic, but he just keeps punching it into me like a maniac, my belly is a bell and this monstrous clapper keeps striking against it, I can feel my vagina now against the abdominal wall, as if the thing is going to burst through my skin near the navel, I never imagined it was possible to go so far, so high, in such an unknown and unthinkable direction. The thing keeps right on, relentlessly, as if it has a life of its own. At last I let myself go and cry out, I cry that I'm afraid, afraid, afraid. My vagina is on fire, my mucous membranes consumed by the flames, the clapper and the bell have become one inside me, tolling with the urgency of an alarm. Soon it will be too late, the entire landscape will be razed to the ground, laid waste for ever. In a last violent reflex of survival, at the limits of pain and exhaustion, my muscles rebel, my knees lift, my back arches, I wriggle like an eel, and the thing slips out and lands against my thigh, still twitching uselessly.

The eyes of my kittens are half-open, though still sticky at the corners. I'm reminded of the red-headed man's sperm.

He phoned. I said: 'It's over.'

And he said: 'Just knowing you exist, just knowing I could have a drink with you from time to time would be enough.'

'All right,' I said. 'I don't mind a drink.'

The blood has stopped. I miss it. It was bright and very pure, quite unlike menstrual blood. It was the kind of blood you see in old paintings of Christ on the cross and the Virgin of the Seven Sorrows.

We have our drink on a café terrace. It's a fine day, the sky looks as if it's been given a thorough cleaning. I tell myself I'm not going to any more hotel rooms. Summer's coming and I love the sun. I don't want to sacrifice any of my afternoons while the weather's fine. I'll work at the travel agency in the mornings as usual, advising people who think that going away gives you a new lease of life, and then in the afternoons I can be alone in the woods. I tell myself that Gilles likes to come with me to the woods and make love against a tree. I tell myself that the sun will help me to say no.

I say yes. We're going to see each other again. Somewhere else. In another hotel. That way I'll be sure of you, the man says. I've said yes and now I feel even more disgusted. But it's good. It means he's bound to notice how unbearable it is for me. My body will reject him once and for all, in a way my will never could.

At home, I've been watching my cat, Douce. Since the kittens started to open their eyes, she's been going out into the garden for longer periods, then coming back for a nap on my bed. She used to be so submissive, now she's becoming dominant. I've seen her provoking the stray ginger tom who comes into my bedroom and lolls shamelessly on the unmade bed. He lies there and watches Douce advance. They look each other up and down. He waits for her to beat a retreat, but she growls and throws herself on him. He runs off. She's surprised to see him go. Then she notices how rumpled the sheet is where they were fighting and she crawls back in terror from the strange swelling in her resting place.

I put on a very short, figure-hugging dress. I'm past the age for it, but that's the way it is. Things end, but you drink them to the last drop, without understanding why. Gilles is coming back. He says I'm beautiful like this, with nothing on underneath.

Gilles takes me to the woods. All we have is two hours. As we stroll, we talk. About everything except the red-headed man. Gilles doesn't touch me. He smokes as he walks. I'm fascinated by the way he smokes, the way he screws up his eyes slightly. It makes him look gentle and hard at the same time. He's somewhere else, somewhere far from me. He moves away as he smokes, breathing in the whole world through the smoke, a world from which I am temporarily excluded. It's a respite from me, his temptress. He smokes, delivered to my gaze, absorbed in a pleasure that has nothing to do with me. This is how I possess him when he escapes me, with the intense longing I feel as I contemplate his beauty across the distance created between us by the cigarette he holds between his fingers. He has long hands, with well-groomed nails. When I think of his fingers, two images come to mind: a long, thin cigarette, and my swollen vulva.

He walks and smokes, and we talk. Time passes, an hour, I don't ask anything. I'm surprised he hasn't laid me down in the bracken like last time. I look at him questioningly. With an air of mystery, he turns and starts to walk back the way we came.

'Aren't you going to do anything to me?' I'm quite cool, quite unconcerned. 'Yes,' he says, 'everything . . . ' All at once, my belly becomes heavy and hot, pulling me so strongly in a downward direction that I'm already weak at the knees. We go on a little further and I can hardly walk. He points to a tree that's not like the others, a chestnut tree surrounded by beeches. I lean my back against it. Gilles lifts my dress and with infinite gentleness begins to use his hands on me.

'Your cunt swells like a fruit,' he says, as admiring as ever.

I too can feel the fruit swelling, filling with juice at a dizzying rate, getting huge, oozing—what strange power my lover's hand has to bring such a flat, dry fruit to ripeness so quickly, to fill it in an instant with hot liquid and the desire to be picked or to explode under the exquisite pressure of his fingers. I explode, my knees give way against the trunk, my head goes back and the bark catches my hair, pulling it like a hand.

'You're a fast finisher,' Gilles says.

My breath gradually slows, stretching down to my feet. I straighten up, my back against the tree, my flesh melting into it. Being different from the others gives the tree an authority that fills me with strength, and I feel strengthened too by my cry, which ascended all the way up the trunk to the sky, to the thin clouds streaked by the topmost branches. I open Gilles's flies, plunge my hand inside his pants and take out his cock. Gilles gets a hard-on as soon as he touches me, sometimes even just thinking of me when I'm far away. When that happens, it makes him want to cry: I know, because he told me. Now, like a child, he puts himself in my power, letting my hands move back and forth, back and forth, and very soon I can sense he's about to come, so I undo the buttons that go up the front of my dress like a ladder and expose my naked and swollen belly and Gilles moans and comes over my skin. I peer down at the bright gel that covers my dark pubic hair and I laugh, it's so tepid and pure and milky inside, every time I move it quivers. It's like the gel they put on the bellies of pregnant women before they have a scan. I remember going to the hospital with my sister when she was eight months pregnant, her white skin stretched to breaking point, the male nurse applying the gel, then the probe gliding and turning over her belly. I can still see the shape of the baby swimming on the screen, stretching. You were supposed to marvel at the sight of an arm, a leg, a tiny cock, a heart beating regularly, but I couldn't make out anything so precise. All I saw were moving life-forms vaguer than dreams, than all my dreams of motherhood, indecipherable oceanic forms that bring tears to your eyes.

The spores of the ferns are sticking to my belly like gold dust, and Gilles tells me how beautiful I am, how very beautiful.

When I see the red-headed man again, we're on the train going to town, the white lines of the platform rushing past us. He takes a quick look at me in my very short dress and tells me he'd like to be going out with a 'real looker', so people passing would turn round and envy him, but there are beautiful girls who are nothing much in bed and others who . . . I don't feel angry at what he's saying. I'm only surprised that Gilles thinks I'm so beautiful. I tell myself that he's wrong and this man is right. It's time I realized I'll never be a 'real looker'.

The weather is radiant. On the embankments on either side of the railway line, spruces sway like ivory umbrellas. I wonder suddenly why I'm going to shut myself away again behind closed curtains with this man. The one consolation is that it'll soon be over. But I know I'm being unfaithful. To the sun, to the woods, to my solitude, to the empty times that only Gilles can fill. I'm going to waste two hours of my life. A hole, a stain that will dirty the trees, the sun, Gilles's love for me, and everything I've ever learned or ever will learn about love.

The red-headed man is talking without looking at me, staring down at the little table where I've placed my elbow to support my chin with my hand.

'I'd be happy to get what you don't give your boyfriend.'

Without thinking, I reply that it's not like that, everybody's 'unique'; he can give me what no other man can: blows, unrestrained violence, violence without love, that more than anything, without love. It's so refreshing not to love, if you only knew—you do know, don't you?

Then I stop, disconcerted to see him look up at me with the eyes of a devoted dog who is resigned to being constantly abandoned. And it occurs to me that it's not just the absence of love. What this man also gives me is the obscenity of his distress, the absence of light and creativity and joy in everything he does. His sadness is so absolute, it fascinates me and wounds me at the same time, it opens me more surely than any scalpel could, making me a bundle of exposed nerves, of bared entrails with my cunt throbbing and quivering in the middle, a red gaping mouth crying out for ever at the pain of the blows. I tell myself that the red-headed man could be our dog, Gilles's and mine, he could be a dog that belongs to everybody, a dog that collects scraps from under the table; anyway I've always dreamed of being fucked by an animal. The thought of it makes me feel suddenly lethargic and there's a slight trembling in my voice as I ask: 'Are we there yet?'

There are no more stops, we're nearly there, the man says. And a great hole opens beneath me, and the vibration of the wheels penetrates me in a gentle and regular rhythm in time with the throbbing of my cunt. My body is preparing itself. I remember waking up last night, well before dawn, with the kind of feverish excitement you feel at the anticipation of sexual pleasure, though I wasn't anticipating any pleasure, though I had no hope of it. All I could think of was the pain to come. I was waiting for it, like a giant spruce tree, a poisonous hemlock spruce growing for some reason on a railway embankment. I looked down at the whiteness of my body, the limbs I couldn't help stretching, and the cunt I could no longer bring myself to touch, as if it carried death inside it. I couldn't get back to sleep after that. I waited for the sky to brighten. It was a long night, and I was nothing but an inflamed belly, crying out in solitude and expectation.

We're there. It's another hotel, smaller this time. An ordinary, two-storey, red-brick suburban house. There's a tall, well-built man perched on a ladder in the yard next door, cutting scrap metal with a blowtorch. He stops for a moment and turns to look at us, staring as we go round to the back door of the red house. I can feel his eyes on me, that man cutting metal, that man with fire at the end of his arm, a dazzling fire that you can't look at directly. I look down at the ground, pursued by that blinding gaze. He knows exactly why I'm wearing a short dress and how long it'll be before I come out again. I feel very weak, suddenly, under the pressure of those eyes bending me and shaping me like molten metal. The red-headed man rings the doorbell. A little dog barks. The door is opened by a fat woman, who leads us into an old-fashioned kitchen. She is in the middle of doing her ironing.

Her linen is on the ironing board. The dog sniffs at my calves.

'The price includes a drink,' the fat woman says. She's wearing an acid-green skirt and a spotted blouse.

We turn down the drink and go upstairs. The staircase is narrow and dark and echoes to our steps. The room is very small, almost an attic, with a bed at floor level and paper peeling from the wall, paper with big gold flowers on a red background.

'Get undressed. Lie down.'

I'm used to the orders by now; I feel as if I was born to take orders. I lie on the bed. The bedspread smells of other people, an indefinable mixture of secretions. I get up and tear it off. Beneath it, the sheets are clean and cool to the touch when I lie down again. I suddenly have a strong desire to sleep.

'Spread your legs.'

Shyly, I mention the blood, and my bad night. The man says he'll be gentler this time. Maybe he too has been affected by the way the man next door looked at us, or troubled by the brightness of the blowtorch in the solar forge of the afternoon. Brightness on brightness. But there's no brightness here inside the room, the curtains stifle the light just as they will muffle any cries. The man doesn't put pegs on my breasts or whip me. He penetrates me with his fingers and digs about inside for a long time, more calmly than before. He asks me if my boyfriend has ever fucked me up the arse, and if so, how many times. Just once, I tell him in a low voice, and it hurt.

'Get down on all fours.'

I do as he says.

'It's obvious you're not used to it,' he says. 'You need widening. Next time we'll start with that.'

I don't react. But what I'm thinking is: There won't be a next time, you idiot, you'll never see me again, me or my arsehole. So work on me all you want, one last time . . . That's what he does, methodically, with an object I haven't had a chance to examine, something long and not too wide, which simply forces a little entry, then goes further and deeper. I can feel it beating against the wall separating the two cavities of my belly, I get the impression it's going to burst through the wall into my vagina and come out the other side, in a stream of blood mixed with excrement. It doesn't hurt. The only thing that hurts is the shame of being purged like a mare, I'm melting with shame and abandon, afraid of what could come out, what could spurt in his face when he takes out his contraption and spread over the bed and make the room stink, the room and the whole world, and make me a woman people avoid or spit at as they close their eyes and hold their noses. But my boyfriend, who's interested in everything, my boyfriend, my lover, he'll be next after you, you poor fool, and he'll take advantage of the opening you're making. With his hard, gentle cock, he'll come and go, deep inside me, as far as he can, and he won't be afraid of causing me the pain I felt the first time.

There always has to be a first time, and I was the one who wanted it. I asked Gilles to kneel behind me, got down on all fours, spread my buttocks myself with my tense hands and went in search of his erect cock. In my haste, I impaled myself with such force that I screamed in pain and slid on to my side, bringing my knees up to my chest. Spellbound by what was happening, Gilles passively followed my movement. I sobbed without tears and he said nothing, still motionless inside me. Then, when the pain stopped, I asked him to move, and he did, gently at first, then more quickly, and it didn't hurt any more, or only a little, only as much as it had to. I was still lying on my right side when I felt a cramp in my left leg. I asked Gilles to change position. I expected him to come out, but he stayed inside, taking me by the shoulders and tipping me gently on to him. My back was against his chest and belly, my face was turned to the sky, and his cock stood upright inside me like a pivot. He began to move slowly up and down, thrusting ever so gently into me, cradling me in his great body, my arms hanging loose on either side of us. I was on the crest of a wave, drifting ecstatically, conscious of offering the sun a spectacle of overwhelming beauty.

There's nothing beautiful about the red-headed man or what he's doing to me. I like it this way, I like the way this man's violence accentuates Gilles's gentleness, I like the way his dry, shrill voice makes Gilles's throaty voice ring in my ears, that slightly cracked voice which is the background music of all my emotions; I like the way his brutality deprives me of an orgasm, punishes me where I sin, a depraved little girl whipped for her depravity. That's what I tell myself as he forages inside me and I moan with my head in the pillow. That's what I tell myself in all my humiliation. Gilles has my orgasm, Gilles has it all.

The red-headed man has stopped. Now he's kissing the back of my neck and my shoulders, with precise little pecks. I'm astonished. I wonder what these kisses mean, and the gestures that go with them, the gestures of a timid adolescent confronted by a girl's naked body, yet manic in their frenzy. This is no lover's frenzy, though. The man has no intention of losing himself in me.

'You always stay in control, don't you?' I ask, hating him.

'Always.'

He turns me over, with one hand, spreads my legs and puts his fingers into me. I'm streaming. He laughs.

'You get really wet,' he says. 'Here, taste.'

And he sticks his fingers in my mouth. I don't want to do it. His fingers disgust me, even with the taste of me on them. I hold my breath and the man notices. Suddenly his teeth start to chatter as if he's cold, his features contort alarmingly, he slaps me hard across the face several times and his teeth knock together. It's a terrifying noise, terrifying and fascinating at the same time. There's something wrong with this man, he's mad, the noise indicates the onset of his madness, the noise and the blows which are getting more and more violent, following each other in a hellish rhythm, sending my head spinning from side to side. Suddenly, it all stops. The man gives a little growl and returns to my vulva. He plunges his fingers deep inside again, then gives them to me, demanding that I lick them one by one. Holding my breath, I lick, and despite my disgust I notice how sharp the taste is, like the sweat of a dying person. Could it be that such fluids taste of the emotions that make them flow?

The red-headed man has put his head between my legs. He has his tongue in the streaming furrow, as if he's drinking. He drinks the way an exhausted animal drinks, not pausing to take a breath and yet savouring every last drop. Apart from this wet sound, there's a vast silence, the silence of a savannah, of a desert. On my cheeks, I can feel the heat of his slaps, like two suns. The thrusts of his tongue are precise and pitiless and unerring. My cunt anticipates them, my cunt has become a mouth, transformed into thirsty taste buds. My mind, too, anticipates his tongue, my mind has been washed free of all fear, it walks on the water, barefoot, like a young god newly awoken, and my cunt eats it, then listens to the throbbing of its tiny heartbeat, a fragile little lamp in its red receptacle. All my existence is there, just as the calm surface of a lake only exists through the sky. The rest of my body has vanished, a neutral landscape, a sterile dune. My body has become empty and inert and useless. But my cunt is still howling silently, on the verge of coming, not with that exquisite torture I sometimes feel, which makes me beg for it to be over, but with a gentleness that eternity itself could not exhaust, like the submissiveness of a wild animal brought to its knees, an animal that will not move for centuries. When the orgasm arrives—I'm no longer expecting it, I'm past desire and past hunger—it's nothing like the explosion that startles Gilles, when my limbs go stiff and I cry out as if I'm being broken in two. This is smooth and noiseless, it arches me in a single unbroken wave, and billions of tiny drops of sea water unite in my veins and on my skin, at the centre of my muscles and my nerves. I come like a saint in her ecstasy, radiantly, lips parted in a smile, suffused with a sweetness beyond words.

'Well, well,' the man says, 'I thought you were asleep.'

I open my eyes. He no longer has that twisted look on his face, when his muscles protrude and his eyes disappear. His eyes are weary now, and very blue, and his flesh is tender and glistening with sweat. He lies down next to me and relaxes into stillness. His body is like a child's, narrow and white, and his sweat is light as water and has no taste. I drink at the surface of his skin, like a child at its mother's breast.

When we emerge from the red house, the man with the blowtorch looks at us again, and this time I don't lower my eyes. I'm carrying my orgasm like a pregnant woman her belly, and I want to be shown respect. □

Translation by HOWARD CURTIS

96

GRANTA

LUC SANTE
LINGUA FRANCA

Luc Sante the day before his fifth birthday

In order to write of my childhood I have to translate. It is as if I were writing about someone else. As a boy, I lived in French; now, I live in English. The words don't fit, because languages are not equivalent to one another. If I say, 'I am a boy; I am lying in my bed; I am sitting in my room; I am lonely and afraid,' attributing these thoughts to my eight-year-old self, I am being literally correct but emotionally untrue. Even if I submit the thoughts to indirect citation and the past tense I am engaging in a sort of falsehood. I am playing ventriloquist, and that eight-year-old, now made of wood and with a hinged jaw, is sitting on my knee, mouthing the phrases I am fashioning for him. It's not that the boy couldn't understand those phrases. It is that in order to do so, he would have to translate, and that would mean engaging an electrical circuit in his brain, bypassing his heart.

If the boy thought the phrase, 'I am a boy', he would picture Dick or Zeke from the school books, or maybe his friends Mike or Joe. The word 'boy' could not refer to him; he is *un garçon*. You may think this is trivial, that *garçon* simply means 'boy', but that is missing the point. Similarly, *maman* and *papa* are people; 'mother' and 'father' are notions. *La nuit* is dark and filled with fear, while 'the night' is a pretty picture of a starry field. The boy lives in *une maison* with a house on either side. His *coeur* is where his feelings dwell, and his heart is a blood-pumping muscle. For that matter, his name is Luc, pronounced *lük*; everybody around, though, calls him 'Luke', which is an alias, a mask.

He regards the English language with a curiosity bordering on the entomological. Watching the *Amerloques* moving around in their tongue is like seeing lines of ants parading through tunnels, bearing sections of leaves. He finds it funny, often enough. In school, for instance, when nutrition is discussed, the elements of a meal are called 'servings', a word that always conjures up images of footmen in claw-hammer coats bearing covered dishes. Since he knows that his classmates, however prosperous their parents might be, aren't likely to have servants, he substitutes the familiar advertising icon of Mother entering the room with a trussed turkey on a platter, which is no less alien or ridiculous. He gathers that this scene has some material basis in the lives of Americans, although it appears to him contrived beyond belief. American life, like the English language, is fascinating and hopelessly phoney.

His vantage point is convenient, like a hunter's blind. He has some struggles with the new language—it will be years, for example, before his tongue and teeth can approximate the 'th' sound, and in the meantime he will have to tolerate laughter every time he pronounces 'third' as 'turd'—but at the same time he is protected. No one will ever break his heart with English words, he thinks. It is at home that he is naked. If the world outside the door is a vast and apparently arbitrary game, inside lies the familiar, which can easily bruise or cut him. No, his parents aren't monsters, nothing like that, although they may not appreciate their own power. Anyway, he has raised and nurtured enough monsters by himself to inflict pain without need of assistance. The French language is a part of his body and his soul, and it has a latent capacity for violence. No wonder he has trouble navigating between the languages at first: they are absurdly different, doors to separate and unequal universes. Books might allege they are the same kind of item, like a pig and a goat, but that is absurd on the face of it. One is tissue and the other is plastic. One is a wound and the other is a prosthesis.

Of course, the French language would not be so intimate, wrenching, and potentially dangerous to him if he had remained in a French-speaking world. There he would be bombarded by French of all temperatures, flavours, connotations. His friends, his enemies, his teachers, his neighbours, the newspaper, the radio, the billboards, people on the street, pop songs, movies, assembly instructions, lists of ingredients, shouting drunks, mumbling lunatics, indifferent officials, all would transmit in French. Pretty girls would speak French. He would pick up slang, poesy, academese, boiler-plate, specialized jargon, cant, nonsense. He would not only hear French everywhere but absorb it unconsciously all the time. He would learn the kind of things no dictionary will tell you: for example that apparent synonyms are in reality miles apart, each with its own calluses of association. By and by, *je* would become more than his private self, would find itself shoulder to shoulder with the *je* of a million others. There would be traffic and commerce between inner life and outer world. A great many things would go without saying, be taken for granted. It would seem as though language had arisen from the ground, had always been and would always be.

Instead French festers. It is kept in darkness and fed meagrely by the spoonful. It isn't purposely neglected, of course; there is nothing intentionally punitive about the way it is sequestered and undernourished. On the contrary: it is cherished, cosseted, rewarded for just being, like an animal in a zoo. But like that animal it can only enjoy a semblance of its natural existence. Its memory of the native habitat grows sparser all the time, and its attempts at normality become play-acting, become parody, become rote. Its growth has been stunted, and it correspondingly retains many infantile characteristics. Even as the boy grows gradually tougher and more worldly in English, he carries around a French internal life whose clock has stopped. He is unnaturally fragile, exaggeratedly sensitive in his French core. Not surprisingly, he resents this, wants to expunge it, destroy it, pour salt on its traces to prevent regeneration.

What does this say about the boy's view of his family circumstances? That is a complicated matter. French is his soul, and it is also a prison, and the same terms could be applied to his family. At home he is alone with his parents; no one else exists. It is stifling and comforting in equal measure. Out in the world he is entirely alone. He is terrified but he is free. Or potentially free, anyway; he's too young to know. But one of the things that sustains him in the world is the knowledge of his French innards. He can feel superior about it (his peers don't possess anything equivalent, and they'll never have any idea what it feels like) but it is simultaneously a source of shame. At home he may be alone with his parents, but while they have an awesome power over his infant core, his growing English self is something they don't know and can't touch. You can take all these propositions as mathematical equations. Work them out, forwards or backwards, and you will always arrive at the same reduction, the same answer: he is alone.

My attempt to put any sort of words in the boy's mouth is doomed. He doesn't yet have a language. He has two tongues: one is all quivering, unmediated, primal sensation, and

101

the other is detached, deliberate, artificial. To give a full accounting he would have to split himself in two. But I don't know whether I might not have to do the same myself, here and now. To speak of my family, for example, I can hardly employ English without omitting an emotional essence that remains locked in French, although I can't use French, either, unless I am willing to sacrifice my critical intelligence. Could I, employing English, truly penetrate my parents' decision to emigrate? I was born in Verviers, in south-eastern Belgium, birthplace of everyone bearing my last name for at least 800 years. The city was dominated by its textile industry for nearly a millennium, but that industry began to die in the 1950s, and my father was out of a job, and no others were to be had. The notice of bankruptcy of my father's employer was posted in French; the agonized conversations between my parents were conducted in French; the war bride and her brother, my father's childhood friends, invited my parents to consider joining them in New Jersey, phrasing their inducements in French. I now understand such grave adult matters, but I understand them in English. A chasm yawns between languages, between my childhood and my present age. But there is an advantage hidden in this predicament: French is an archaeological site of emotions, a pipeline to my infant self. It preserves the very rawest, deepest, least guarded feelings.

If I stub my toe, I may profanely exclaim, in English, 'Jesus!' But in agony, such as when I am passing a kidney stone, I might cry, *'Petit Jésus!'* with all the reverence of nursery religion. Others have told me that when I babble in feverish delirium or talk in my sleep, I do so in French. Preserved, too, in French, is a world of lost pleasures and familial comforts. If someone says, in English, 'Let's go visit Mr and Mrs X,' the concept is neutral, my reaction is determined by what I think of Mr and Mrs X. On the other hand, if the suggestion is broached in French, *'Allons dire bonjour'*, the phrasing affects me more powerfully than the specifics. *'Dire bonjour'* calls up a train of associations: for some reason I see my great-uncle Jules Stelmes, dead more than thirty years, with his fedora and his enormous white moustache and his soft dark eyes. I smell coffee and the raisin bread called *cramique*, hear the muffled bong of a parlour clock and the repetitive commonplaces of chit-chat in the drawling accent of the Ardennes, people rolling their Rs and leaning hard on their initial Hs. I feel a rush-caned chair under me, see white curtains and a starched tablecloth, can almost tap my feet on the cold ceramic tiles, maybe the *trompe l'oeil* pattern that covered the entire floor surface of my great-uncle Albert Remacle's farmhouse in Viville. I am sated, sleepy, bored out of my mind.

The triggers that operate this mechanism are the simplest, humblest expressions. They are things that might be said to a child or said often within a child's hearing. There are common comestibles: *une tasse de café, une tartine, du chocolat.* There are interjections and verbal place-markers: *sais-tu, figure-toi, je t'assure, mon Dieu.* And, naturally, there are terms of endearment. In my family, the use of someone's first name was nearly always an indication of anger or a prelude to bad news. My parents addressed me as *fifi, chou* (cabbage), *lapin* (rabbit), *vî tchèt* (meaning 'old cat' in Walloon, the native patois of southern Belgium), *petit coeur.* If I'd done something mischievous, my father would laugh and call me *cûrêye* (Walloon for 'carcass' or 'spavined horse'—like saying, 'you're rotten'); if I'd made myself especially comfortable, such as by taking up most of the couch, he'd shake his head and grin and call me *macrale* (Walloon for 'witch'). I regularly got called *tièsse èl aîr* (head in the clouds; Walloon). If my mother was teasing me in mock anger, she'd call me a *petit chenapan* (little scamp); if it was my father, he'd be likely to say *'t'es ô tièssetou'* ('you're a stubborn one', in Walloon). My father's real anger was rare and grave; my mother's boiled over quickly even if it faded just as fast. She might call me a *vaurien* (good-for-nothing) or a *sale gosse* (dirty kid), an *èstèné* (an idiot, literally 'bewildered'; Walloon) or a *singlé* (a simpleton) or a *nolu* (a nullity; Walloon). If I'd really stung her, though, she'd yell *chameau!* (camel), and I liked that, because she was acknowledging I had some kind of power. There are worse words, which still have the capacity to make me cringe: *cochon* (pig), *crapuleux* (vile, vicious), *crotté* (filthy), *mâssî* (ditto; Walloon). Those words are woven through the fabric of my early adolescence.

A few years ago, early in the morning, I was waiting to cross a street in Liège. I wasn't quite awake yet, and was lost in thought, so that when I heard someone shout *'Fais attention! Regarde!'* I immediately stiffened. All of a sudden I was back at the age of eight or nine, being reproved by my parents. As it happened, there was a small boy standing next to me, holding a tray of empty coffee cups which he was returning to the café opposite; his father, manning a flea-market booth behind us, had observed the kid putting a toe into the street unmindful of oncoming traffic. It can easily happen to me, when faced with some officious francophone creep, shopkeeper or librarian or customs agent, that I lose thirty years and two feet off my height. If I haven't briefed myself beforehand, I crumple. This can happen even though I've kept my French alive internally through reading, as well as occasional conversations with friends. But even in such circumstances I can find myself tripped up, suddenly sprawled. I can be reading something truly scabrous, something by Georges Bataille, say, turning the pages as an imperturbable adult, and then a turn of phrase will shock me, not some description of outlandish vice but rather a perfectly innocent locution lying in the midst of the smut. It will throw everything else into a new relief. Suddenly it is as if one of my aunts had looked up from her coffee and started spewing obscenities.

Since I live almost entirely in English now, I can regard French with some of the same detachment and sense of the ridiculous with which I once regarded my adopted tongue. If I walk into an American discount store and the loudspeaker starts braying 'Attention shoppers!' I will consign the noise to the realm of static, switch off its ability to reach me except as an irritant. On the other hand, if I am in a Belgian supermarket and the loudspeaker begins its recital, nearly always in a polished female murmur rather than the American male bark: *'Monsieur, madame, nous vous conseillons . . . '* I am bemused, imagining the rapport between the voice and its sleek, well-dressed target, someone so exquisitely put together that he or she can purchase low-fat frozen entrées with a withering superiority, as if picking out a *grand cru classé*. I am never the 'you' of American advertising because I consciously slam the door, but in French I am never given the opportunity to spurn the come-on. I am excluded at the gate. Naturally there is a class factor involved—in French I revert to proletarian status as easily as to childhood—but the exclusion is also due to my status as a counterfeit Belgian, an American pretender.

I can cross the border between English and French, although I can't straddle it. Years ago, when I worked behind the cash register in a store, I resented the demands of the customers and sometimes went out of my way to be rude to them, to put them in their place. After work, though, I might go to some other shop, and there, trying to find out whether the shirt came in a larger size or a darker colour, would find myself resenting the arrogance and apathy of the clerks. I had jumped from one side of the fence to the other. I could no more simultaneously occupy the mentality of clerk and client than I could bat a ball to myself in the outfield. Each claim effaced the other. It was useless to try and apportion blame; customers and clerks were both rude and both justified, were in fact interchangeable. This insight is perhaps the closest I've ever got to understanding the psychology that lies behind nationalism. The situation is a bit like one of the famous optical illusions, in which the silhouettes of two facing profiles form the outline of a vase. You can see the vase, and then you can see the profiles, but you can't see both images at once.

Belgium is an ill-fitting suit of a country. Stitched together from odds and ends, it represents a purely strategic decision on the part of the larger powers to create a nation state. It unnaturally couples two language groups (actually three language groups if you include the relatively untroubled German-speaking minority—no more than 70,000 souls in any case), and both have ambiguous ongoing relationships with the majority stockholders of their languages, i.e. the Dutch and the French. The Flemish and the Dutch in recent years have been forming cultural and trade partnerships, and apparently enjoying themselves at it. Their mutual history is somewhat more vexed, with the Dutch regarding the Flemings with a certain benign hauteur, and the Flemish viewing the Dutch as worldly, as apostates, as lacking in seriousness, not to mention virtue. But they read each other's literatures, and just as the Flemings have adopted the grammar and usage of their cousins, so the Dutch appreciate the particular flavour of Flemish expressions, and have helped themselves to dashes of the idiom. Between the Walloons and the French the situation is less comfortable. Essentially, the French feel superior and the Walloons oblige them by feeling embarrassed. There has long been a Francophile segment of the Walloon population, and, as the national tension has risen, so has the noise emitted by a certain minority that favours the detachment of Wallonia from Belgium and its adherence to France. The French have shown no corresponding interest in acquiring five impoverished and déclassé eastern provinces.

The language reflects this French superiority and Belgian embarrassment. Popular manuals for the identification and eradication of *belgicismes* have been published since at least the eighteenth century. Today *Le Soir*, out of Brussels, has a weekly feature that reiterates the same cautions. When speaking of buttered bread say *beurrée*, not *tartine*; and so forth. That example might serve to demonstrate that the wish to eliminate native expressions has nothing to do with grammatical rigour or the rectification of ambiguities, but is merely the expression of a class-bound shame. Visitors always note that Belgians say *septante* for seventy and *nonante* for ninety, whereas the French say *soixante-dix* and *quatre-vingt-dix* respectively. I have no idea why Belgians do not also say *octante* for eighty, the three simpler expressions having been used by French-speaking proletarians of both lands for centuries; the arithmetical puzzles are owed entirely to class pretension. A more recent example of this tendency is what happened across the country to the name of the establishments that make and sell fried potatoes. For untold decades and throughout my childhood they were known as *fritures*, until at some point in the 1970s a humourless functionary decreed the name incorrect, since *friture* is the word for the fat in which the potatoes are fried. Now only establishments older than twenty-five or so years can continue to name themselves that way; the more recent shops must be called *friteries*.

The French, particularly through the agency of their Academy, have long policed their language in such petty ways. Neologisms and loanwords are forbidden, shifts in grammar and usage swiftly curtailed. French was once a major force in the world, among other things the international language of diplomacy. Those who wonder why it has ceded so much of its power to English need look no further than this wish to preserve a seventeenth-century cadaver. Belgians who submit their language to French rules concede twice over. But the submission is by now traditional; after all Walloons have done a fairly effective job of killing off their own tongue.

Walloon is usually identified as a dialect of French, whereas it derived on its own from the Latin of the Roman legions, and is just as old as the patois of Ile de France, which became the official language. The eleventh edition of the *Encyclopaedia Britannica* in fact identifies it as the northernmost Romance language. I once asked a linguist-translator: What is the line separating a language from a dialect? He replied that the situation could be summed up in a phrase: History is written by the victors. The dialect of Ile de France was the patois of the French kings; it subjugated Walloon as well as Provençal, Norman, Lorrain, Gascon, Picard, Occitan, and so on, and reduced them from languages to dialects. The effect of linguistic imperialism is well described by the great Verviétois philologist Jules Feller (1859–1940) in his *Notes de Philologie wallonne* (1912):

> Political necessity, material interest, constraint, and the moral superiority of the conqueror and his language can create within a single century the troubling phenomenon of a tongue being entirely forgotten by its nation. The first generation does its best to gabble the idiom of the foreign invaders. The second generation, if it be to its advantage, already knows the new language better than the old. The third generation for all practical purposes knows and employs only the new.

Feller uses this model to describe the impact of Latin on the Celto-Germanic population of Gallia Belgica, but it applies just as well to the effect of French upon Walloon over the last century (and, incidentally, it is likewise true of the linguistic process that accompanies immigration). Feller goes on to characterize French as 'a brilliant soldier of fortune in the army of Romance dialects who has become a general', while Walloon is 'a little corps of soldiers, consigned to the fringe of the battalion, who have never gotten the chance to distinguish themselves'.

Walloon might yet have had a chance to develop in the nineteenth century, had the Belgian educational establishment seized the opportunity afforded by the country's independence to teach Walloon in schools. Instead the opposite occurred: steps were taken to suppress the language, and teachers took it as their mission to 'cure' pupils of their native tongue. But Walloon did have its golden age. It was brief, lasting from the mid-1880s until just before the First World War. That period saw an efflorescence of Walloon literature, plays and poems primarily, and the founding of many theatres and periodicals. The New York Public Library possesses a surprisingly large collection of literary works in Walloon, quite possibly the largest outside Belgium, and its holdings are statistically representative of the output. Out of nearly a thousand plays in the collection, only twenty-six were published before 1880 and only twenty-one of them after the First World War. The reasons for this decline remain a mystery; it was not occasioned by the war itself. Literary production occurred at different paces in different cities, but Liège, Verviers, Namur and Charleroi led the pack. At its peak, Walloon literature was like a massive exhalation of breath long held in. It approached—as in the comte de Lautréamont's exhortation—poetry made by all.

Walloon was the household tongue of all the relatives of my grandparents' generation. Their parents in turn might have spoken nothing else; that no one bothered to establish rules for the writing of Walloon until Jules Feller did so at the very beginning of this century, just in time for its decline in currency, partly accounts for the fact that nearly everyone in the family tree before my grandparents' era was illiterate. When I hear Walloon spoken, which is not often, I hear the table talk of countless generations of workers and farmers and their wives; not that I particularly wish to subscribe to notions of collective ethnic memory, but the sound of the language conveys the mentality of its speakers so vividly that it is dense with imprints, like fossils. Hearing old men greet each other—'Bôdjou, Françwès'—can move me nearly to tears. It is the keenest tangible manifestation of what

I've lost, even if it is now pretty much lost to everyone. In my childhood it was already a ghost, if a lively one. My mother's parents ceded to the tenor of their times; they spoke Walloon between themselves but did not teach it to their children and discouraged their bringing bits of it home. My father, on the other hand, grew up in a Walloon-speaking household in a city with a rich Walloon tradition.

Walloon today is the province of the elderly, at least those of the working class or in rural communities, along with a few younger diehards and hobbyists in the cities. Most people regard it with a certain embarrassment, like the memory of a bastard grandsire who ate with his hands. The young, who are media-fixated and thus Parisianized or Americanized, couldn't care less. To me, growing up, it was both familiar and strange. Sometimes my parents reached for an English phrase and came up with a Walloon one instead—the confusion was understandable given the Germanic strain running among Walloon's Latin roots. (An often-told story in my family related how Lucy Dosquet, when her GI suitor arrived looking like a slob, angrily ordered him in Walloon, *'Louke-tu el mireu!'* He understood perfectly, and studied his reflection.) Sometimes my parents said things to each other in Walloon they didn't want me to understand—pertaining to Christmas presents, maybe. I was never taught Walloon, but I had a fair-sized vocabulary anyway (there were concepts I could only express in Walloon; growing pains, for example, were always *crèhioûles*), and I simply absorbed its structure from hearing bits of it from my parents and from hearing my grandparents and great-aunts and great-uncles speak it. I can read it with ease; other applications don't present themselves. Like the lives of my ancestors, Walloon appears humble and yet mighty, elemental and at the same time complex, remote but a part of my fibre. I use what I have of it only internally. It is that sad paradox, a silent tongue.

One of the great stalwarts of Verviétois Walloon in this century was Jean Wisimus (1868–1953) who managed to combine the tasks of textile dealer, newspaper columnist, lexicographer (he compiled the only dictionary of the Verviers tongue that exists), historian, author (of *Dès Rôses èt dès Spènes*—Roses and Thorns—a volume of rather affecting reminiscences of the old

Verviers), and founder and long-time president of Lu Vî Tchène
(The Old Oak), the last major Walloon organization in the city. His
first book, however, published in 1921, was *L'Anglais langue
auxiliaire internationale* (English, the international second
language). Its publication may have been delayed by the war; in
any case he begins by addressing concerns that have a distinctly
pre-1914 air about them. Universal languages were all the rage
then. Dr Zamenhof's Esperanto, Monsignor Schleyer's Volapük,
Sudre's Solresol, Dyer's Lingualumina, Bauer's Spelin, Dornoy's
Balta, Marchand's Dilpok, the Marquis de Beaufort's Ido—all were
supposed to bring about international harmony by tearing down
the tower of Babel and making the crooked ways straight, and all
of them smell like the sort of decorous, idealistic Edwardian science
fiction that was about to be buried in the trenches of Verdun.
Wisimus has no patience at all with such nonsense. 'An artificial
language is like canned food; it's a product without flavour or
aroma.' By contrast there is English, which has the simplest and
most analytical grammar, and furthermore has already invaded
every domain ('you visit the *world's fair*, buy a *ticket*, go to the *bar*,
watch out for *pickpockets* . . . see the *cakewalk*, the *looping-the-
loop, cow-boys* from the *far-west* . . . '). Although some people will
always grumble about its errant spelling, its destiny is clear, and
anyway, *'Un beau désordre est un effet de l'art'* (a beautiful mess is
an artistic effect: Boileau). English, he predicts, will become a
worldwide medium of convenience, like the telephone and the
telegraph. Unless, that is, Japan conquers the planet . . .

Somehow, like some sort of Jules Vernian astronaut, I wound
up making the journey from Wisimus's Verviers into the very heart
of the linguistic future. For my first communion I was presented
with a dictionary whose jacket copy promised it to be 'as up to
date as Telstar!' Two years later I decided I wanted to be a writer,
and having made that decision never thought of writing in any
language but English. It was at hand, it was all new, it was not the
language of my parents, it *was* the language of Robert Louis
Stevenson and Ray Bradbury and the Beatles, it contained a ready-
made incentive to competition, and besides, Mrs Gibbs in the
fourth grade at St Teresa's School in Summit told me I had talent,
and that clinched it. Gradually, I successfully passed myself off as

another being. I was thirteen or fourteen the last time anyone complimented me on my charming accent. English became my rod and my staff, my tool and my weapon, at length my means of making a living. My mask merged with my skin. My internal monologue ever so gradually shifted from French into English; I even began to talk to cats and dogs (who understand all languages) in English. My most intimate conversations came to be conducted in English. Today, when someone addresses me as 'Luke' I respond without a second thought; when I hear *'lük'* I jump as if I've gotten an electric shock. Even though I know better, I feel as if someone had just looked down into my naked soul.

I still speak French with my parents, of course, although French is perhaps a misleading word there, since over the years we've developed a family dialect, a Franglais that is a lot like Spanglish: *'Nous sommes allés chez les séniores citizeunnes,'* my mother will tell me, describing a visit to the local old-folks club, *'et nous avons mangé du cornebif et du cabbage.'* I am almost physically unable to talk to my parents in English, even when they are using the language out of politeness because there is an English speaker present. Talking to my parents in English would be like exchanging nonsensical pleasantries studded with code words, as though we were surrounded by the Gestapo and anxious to give nothing away. Or maybe it would be as if I had invited my parents to a wild party I was throwing for my friends.

I suppose I am never completely present in any given moment, since different aspects of myself are contained in different rooms of language, and a complicated apparatus of airlocks prevents the doors from being flung open all at once. Still, there are subterranean correspondences between the linguistic domains that keep them from stagnating. The classical order of French, the Latin-Germanic high-low dialectic of English, and the onomatopoeic peasant lucidity of Walloon work on one another critically; they help enhance precision and reduce cant. They are all operative, potentially. Given desire and purpose, I could make my home in any of them. I don't have a house, only this succession of rented rooms. That sometimes makes me feel as though I have no language at all, but it also gives me the advantage of mobility. I can leave, anytime, and not be found. □

magazine littéraire

un mensuel exclusivement consacré aux livres et aux écrivains

Colette

un dossier
consacré à un écrivain, une littérature étrangère ou un mouvement d'idées.

toute l'actualité littéraire
en France et à l'étranger. Une centaine de livres recensés, critiqués, analysés chaque mois.

de grands entretiens
avec des romanciers, des poètes, des philosophes, des historiens.

offre spéciale d'abonnement aux lecteurs de Granta 1 an £36
au lieu de £45

magazine littéraire
40, rue des Saints-Pères
75007 Paris – France
tél : 33 1 45.44.14.51
fax : 33 1 45 48 86 36

GRANTA

PIERRE MERLE
WHOOAH . . . PIZZA!

Pierre Merle

The following examples of contemporary French slang come from *Le Dico de l'Argot fin-de-siècle* compiled by a Parisian journalist, Pierre Merle. The dictionary vividly represents the range of influences on French speech: France's immigrant populations, Anglo-American popular culture, technology, the criminal world and the particular French art of *verlan*, backslang, by which words are rearranged according to ever more arcane principles. The Académie française and the French Ministry of Culture keenly disapprove of linguistic imports. Foreign words are given French equivalents—*baladeur* for Walkman, for instance; quotas of French songs are imposed on radio stations, and businesses can be fined if they use too many foreign words, such as 'sandwich', on their shop windows. Slang certainly puts the much-feared 'Anglicization' into perspective, in that French slang actively appropriates Anglo-American words just as often as it passively capitulates to them. In his preface to the *Dico*, however, Claude Duneton makes a different point: several French slang verbs do not have the full range of conjugations and break all the rules of French syntax. 'We are in the presence of a breach,' he writes, 'and only the future will reveal if it is going to threaten our language as it now exists, or simply amount to an amusing phenomenon.' Some of these words may slide out of fashion and disappear; others may well be destined to join the mainstream of French.

accro, hooked on something, dependent. Abbreviation of *accroché*, a literal translation of the American expression 'hooked'. Origin: drug jargon in the Seventies. You can be *accro* on *zan, zen, zob* (liquorice, zen or dick) or anything you want.

acter, play a role, act. Common in film world. Generally: take action.

afnaf, from the English 'half-and-half'. Since about 1950.

after, a bar, club or place to finish off an evening and see the night through until dawn. For instance, the Bar du Potager, rue de la Grande-Truanderie, Paris. More broadly: a bar and club crawl that leaves you 'wrecked'.

after eight, blow job. From the English brand of chocolates filled with mint cream, which are specifically marketed as an after-dinner treat. *'Allez, tu m'f'rais pas un petit after eight vite fait, là?'* 'Come on, give us a quick little after eight!'

airbags, 1. Breasts. *'Putain, les airbags qu'elle a!'* 'Jeez! Check out the airbags on that!' 2. Someone (girl or transvestite) possessing these fabulous attributes.

airpro, good in every respect, someone you can trust. *'Il est très airpro!'* A compression of the French expression: to have a professional air.

allumer les bougies (to light candles), explain oneself, develop one's arguments, in traditional and probably eternal slang. *'Bon allez! On allume les bougies maintenant!'* 'Right then! Let's light some candles!'

arglais, neologism denoting the mixture of slang and English, similar to the neologism *Franglais*, which was invented by the journalist Roger Minne in 1951 during an interview with Raymond Rouleau in New York. Example: *'C'est un mec au look cool, ni hectic ni skin, ni flippant, le bon pote avec qui y a tout de suite le feeling bonnard.'* 'He's cool, he's not wired or a nutter and he doesn't get freaked out, he's a good guy, you click with him straight away.' The rock world and the press are great consumers of *arglais*, as is rap.

avoir l'oreille Van Gogh (to have Van Gogh's ear), to have stayed on the phone too long. Astonishing cultural reference, which appeared around the centenary of the master's death in 1990.

baby-krach, the contemporary decline in the Western birth rate. The opposite of the post-war baby boom.

bail, money, in the language of the young. Transliteration of the English 'buy'. *'T'as du bail?'* 'Are you cashed up?'

barbecue, device for 'estimating the speed of a vehicle', as the police say. Good for grilling speedsters.

bavard (chatterbox), answering machine. Partly because callers rarely manage to keep their messages short. But also, perhaps, because of its basic function of reeling off messages. Formerly: a lawyer.

breaker (pronounced *bréquer*), 1. Take a break, take a rest. 2. *'Breaker un jeune talent'* (showbiz talk) means, as a representative of Sony Music pointed out one day on television, discover a young talent and give him or her their 'break'.

bullshiter, to bullshit, to have someone on, to talk rubbish.

Camembert, important figure, big shot. Translation of 'big cheese', the Anglo-American equivalent to the French *une grosse légume*. Heard at EuroDisney on its opening day, 11 April 1992.

c'est glitter!, it's great, superb and, above all, showy. *'Glitter, tes chouzes!'* 'Your shoes are really something!' From the English 'to glitter'.

115

Pierre Merle

c'est l'hallu!, I can't believe my eyes! Tends to rival, especially among the young, the very common *'J'hallucine!'* Comes at the end of a phrase, and expresses surprise in both a good and a bad sense.

chéwam (pronounced *chéouame*), at my house, *chez moi*, in backslang. *'Chéwam ou chéwat?'* 'My place or yours?'

chouzes, from the English, shoes. More often for show than for walking.

clandax, illegal immigrant (young). *'Chez les grossistes y a un max de clandax!'* 'The wholesaler's is full of illegals!' (heard at a bistro in Les Halles in Paris). You can also say *clandos*, which similarly comes from the French *clandestin*.

dico, intellectual, or, more ironically, someone who always knows everything. *'Mais oui, c'est ça, t'es le méga-dico, toi!'* 'Oh yes, that's right, you're the mega-egghead round here!' From 'dictionary', of course.

dose (or *dosé*), *être dose* is to be a fan of, to be crazy about someone or something.

faire basket, to leave quickly and without further ado. Possibly from *les baskets*: originally basketball shoes, now any sort of trainers, and hence ideal for making a quick getaway. *'Comment qu'j'ai fait basket!'* 'I was out of there!'

faire cheese, to smile. First used to make people smile for a photograph. Still very common, especially among the young.

faire une mayonnaise, to launch oneself into a long, meandering electric guitar solo. *'La mayonnaise qu'il a faite!'* 'He rocked!' (heard at an Eric Clapton concert at Bercy, 21 April 1995). Can simply mean: Liven up the atmosphere. *'Faisons une mayonnaise!'* 'Let's rock this joint!'

fax, flat-chested girl, in young people's speech: *'Sandrine, c'est l'fax total!'* (heard in the Vieux Bistro, near the Edgar-Quinet Lycée in February 1996). Also known as a CD-ROM. In the past, the expression was *planche à pain*: breadboard.

from, name given to those born and bred in France by those born elsewhere. Abbreviation of *fromage blanc*.

go, girl. Probably by abbreviation of the older slang word, *gonzesse*, meaning bird or chick. There may also be a hint of English influence involved, as in 'to go'—'Well, your sister, is she a goer then?'

hach, shame. *'J'ai la hach pour toi!'* 'I'm ashamed of you!' From the Arabic *heichma*.

il peut fumer sous la douche (he can smoke in the shower), he's got a big nose. Not brand new, but still very common.

116

natürlich, Ulrich (or *natürlich, Heinrich*), of course! As appropriate, if not yet as common, as, *'A l'aise, Blaise!'* or *'Tu triques, Patrick!'*

némo, change, backslang of *monnaie*. *'T'as d'la némo, cap'taine?'* 'Got any change, captain?' Request popular among tramps in place Saint-André-des-Arts in the mid-Eighties.

ouala!, I swear. North African origin, now common in the suburbs. *'J'y étais pas, avec eux, ouala j'y étais pas!'* 'I wasn't with them, I swear I wasn't!' (Belleville métro, March 1996).

oualou!, nothing, in Arabic. Very common in the suburbs.

overlooké, eccentric, from the English 'overlook'. Used a lot in 1996.

pagetourner, decide to break with somebody, to stop seeing them. *'Je vais la pagetourner!'* 'I don't want to go out with this girl any more, I'm going to turn over a new leaf.'

parler cash, to be straightforward, frank and to the point. *'Eh, j'parle cash, là!'* 'Right, we're talking the bottom line here!'

passeport, condom. There's no entry without it. Beware illegal immigrants. Very common among the young.

pizza!, warning shouted in the face of imminent danger—going under a bus or out of a window or anything with the potential to leave you flattened. *'Traverser le Sébasto? Houlà . . . Pizza!'* 'Cross the boulevard de Sébastopol? Whooah . . . Pizza!'

plan roots, *faire le plan roots* or *être dans un plan roots* is to be eco-friendly, back to nature, or to act as if you are.

scotché, fixed, being unable 'to peel oneself away'. *'J'ai les yeux scotché sur l'horizon depuis ce matin.'* 'I've been staring at the horizon since this morning.' From Scotch tape, *scotcher* originally means to stick. By extension, *être scotché* is to be amazed, rooted to the spot. *'J'suis scotché!'*, confessed the singer Michel Fugain on television after seeing an Asian singer who could sing in several voices at the same time. *Faire le plan scotche*: stay at home, instead of accepting an invitation.

scuzmi, from the English, excuse me. Young people say *'scuze!'* or *'scouze!'* very often as well.

textile, a clothes wearer, in the language of naturists.

what mille de temps!, an incredibly long time ago! Heard at Servenoble School, Villefontaine (Isère), in March 1996.

zouleur, loser. Backslang of the English word 'loser'. ☐

Translation by WILL HOBSON

AUTUMN 1997

THE STAR FACTORY
CIARAN CARSON

An extraordinary verbal enactment of Belfast by one of Ireland's finest writers. Ciaran Carson remembers and invents the city in which he grew up, as a labyrinth of stories.

Published in hardback at £13.99 · ISBN 186207 - 0725 · November

A TRAITOR'S KISS:
The Life of Richard Brinsley Sheridan
FINTAN O'TOOLE

A portrait of a violent, glittering age and the narrative of a great writer's remarkable career. A major biography by Ireland's leading political and cultural commentator.

Published in hardback at £20.00 · ISBN 186207 - 0261 · October

GRAVITY
ERICA WAGNER

A collection of short stories which mark the debut of a brilliant young writer. Erica Wagner reaches into the fractured, dislocated lives of her characters and finds moments of redemption, despair and exhilaration.

Published in paperback original at £9.99 · ISBN 186207 - 0822 · November

GRANTA

RENE BELLETTO
AGNES

I met Agnès Magellan (a distant relative of the discoverer of new worlds? No, though perhaps a thorough investigation might reveal the contrary) on a train going from Paris to Parris, a small town in Deux-Sèvres which has today lost its name.

Agnès Magellan was a foreigner and could barely put together two words in our language. In spite of that, we became friends easily and soon, feeling that she could trust me, she told me (far less easily, of course) the following story.

For as long as she could remember, she had made her living by illegal means.

Not long ago, a man (of whom she knew nothing, and who had told her nothing about himself) had offered her over the phone a large sum of money simply to be on a certain day at a certain time in a certain café in Paris, dressed in a certain way (short dress, white, with three red circles round the collar), a curly brown wig hiding her blonde hair, her eyebrows painted a very deep black: that is to say, exactly as I saw her now.

A man would come in. He'd walk up to her, he'd look at her, he'd seem disappointed and even angry, he'd ask her questions which she'd obviously be unable to answer, and that was all: he'd leave, and she'd have earned a lot of money for very little effort.

Agnès accepted the assignment, and went to the meeting. A man did indeed appear, looked at her, and was very disappointed. He asked her (in vain) several questions—why was she dressed up like that, who had asked her to do this, did she know the woman she was impersonating, etc; but he didn't become angry. On the contrary: feeling he could trust her, he told her, in spite of the language barrier, the following story.

He was a thief, he said, even though he didn't look at all as one imagines a thief to be.

The night before, he had broken into a wealthy house on the banks of the river, at some distance from the city. He had been about to do his stealing when he had noticed two letters pushed under the door, lying on the floor of the entrance hall. He had opened them and he had read them.

The first, posted in Paris that very morning, was signed by

the owner of the house, informing his wife that he had suddenly decided not to return home that evening. Exhausted by the hell of their life together, he had made up his mind to leave her, even though he loved her, he wrote, as much as ever.

The second letter bore no stamp and no signature. It had been left by a crook, who had kidnapped the lady of the house that very day, shortly after she left the translation bureau in which she worked. To release her, he was demanding a large ransom, which the husband was supposed to leave on the following evening at a certain place and at a certain time, after dressing himself up in a certain fashion (for example, wearing a hat of the sort currently worn in Deux-Sèvres) and walking past a certain café inside which he'd see his wife, safe and sound, waiting for him. But he was not to come near her at that point; if he did, a bullet from an unseen source would strike him dead. He was to pay the ransom money first.

That was why, the thief realized, a disguise was necessary. First of all, so that the wife would not recognize the husband then and there (which might spoil the kidnapper's plan) and secondly, so that the kidnapper (himself or an accomplice) might on the other hand recognize him unmistakably.

After the payment has been made, the husband would take off his disguise, join his wife inside the café, and that would be the end of the story.

The thief searched the house (discovering many photographs of the wife, a beautiful dark-haired woman with deep black eyebrows that gave her eyes a unique depth), pocketed everything he could and left.

On the following morning, he robbed a post office.

And a second one, since the first hadn't been enough.

And in the evening, at the appointed time, he dressed according to the instructions in the letter, carrying a case containing the ransom money. He walked past the café, saw the disguised woman, and went to the designated place to drop off the money. When he returned to the café he went inside and . . .

You can guess the rest. You can also guess the thief's disappointment and bafflement at not finding the woman he expected to find. He asked her (in vain) several questions. He didn't become angry; on the contrary, he told her his story.

Having told his story, the thief had said goodbye to Agnès, regretfully, she thought.

She herself regretted not having called him back. She regretted it very much.

And now, still in her disguise, she was anxiously looking for him. Just before leaving he had mentioned Parris, a small town in Deux-Sèvres where he intended to spend a few days trying to find the key to the mystery (even though the hat typical of that region was a very tenuous link between what he had lived through and what he was now looking for), before returning to Paris.

Agnès had decided to go there too. And from a distance, in the corridors of the train, she had mistaken me for him.

In conclusion, two more points. First, since Agnès, as mentioned before, didn't speak our language, you can imagine the number of mimed scenes, gesticulations, incomprehensible words and straightforward onomatopoeias; the number of sketches trying to clarify the meaning of grimaces, gestures, and voiced sounds—sketches which other grimaces, other gestures and other voiced sounds, or the same ones, attempted in turn to explain—that we needed in order to make ourselves understood. (An even greater number, necessarily and logically, I tell myself with pride, than that which Agnès and the thief had required to communicate in the café where they met.)

Second, I was troubled by the suspicion that the kidnapped woman had perhaps concocted the entire business in order to rob and mortify her husband and, my eyes lost in Agnès's eyes, which no longer left mine, I felt from one instant to the next weak and unhappy, and I dreaded what was about to follow. ☐

Translation by ALBERTO MANGUEL

THE FARM AT LE GARET

Raymond Depardon

Raymond Depardon, the son of a peasant, has become
one of France's most distinguished photojournalists.
He began using a camera when he was ten. His
photographs from that time, which record a rural life
that has vanished, are now the most important to him.

In 1870, my great-grandparents, a young coachman and cook, bought a farm in Arnas in the Beaujolais region of France. Their son, Marius, was born in the following year. He married and had two children—Eugénie and my father, Antoine, who was born on 30 October 1903.

Despite extending the farm, Marius still needed extra meadows for hay, so in 1922 he bought a dilapidated farm in Le Garet, a few kilometres away in the commune of Villefranche-sur-Saône. In 1928 my father moved in, at the age of twenty-five, with his new wife Marthe Bernard. They had spent their honeymoon in Nice and, for a few moments, in Ventimiglia, thanks to the customs men who let them have a little walk on Italian soil. My brother Jean was born in 1938 and I was born in 1942, two years after my father was demobbed. I have few memories of the war. Apparently I took my first steps in the farmyard while you could hear the Allied bombardment.

One day in 1944, during the retreat, some Mongolians came to the farm. They were soldiers from the Eastern Front enlisted into the German army. They asked for two sheep. My father refused. So the soldiers lined my mother, my brother and me against the wall of the barn. They aimed their guns at us. My brother remembers that my mother was crying. A German officer came into the farmyard at that moment and ordered them to stop. Before they left, they took everything anyway.

For a long time at school I was the only child of a peasant in the playground. I'd end up telling the other children, 'If there weren't any peasants, you'd be eating nails!'

The farm, which covered about forty hectares, was in two parts. The top half was crops and the bottom half, which was near the Saône and liable to flood, was livestock and dairy. I'd take the cows and the three horses, Bijou, Fanfan and Robic, to the meadow in the morning and bring them back in the evening. I helped with the haymaking, grape-picking and harvests too. My father had to harvest a hundred sacks of wheat a year, which took two days to bring in. In 1961 he bought a combine harvester, and then it only took two hours.

On Sunday afternoons, my mother forced my father to stop working and come with us to visit our cousins. At about four or five, while we were in one of their kitchens, my father or mother would always say (and I still joke about it), 'This is all very nice but we should be off. We're not from around here.' We'd only be ten kilometres from the farm, sometimes only two or three . . . But I understood. I didn't like staying too long at other people's houses either. I used to miss the farm.

Everyone in my family was either a peasant or a wine merchant. When I was ten, Jean went away to agricultural college and I was given a Lumière camera. My first photographs were of the farm and the animals—calves, cats, horses—but then I began to photograph other things—the small planes that flew from the local airfield, my family and so on. In 1958 I wrote to all the press agencies listed in the Paris phone book and was taken on as a photographer's apprentice. My parents were happy for me, yet they must have been worried: at that time they had no successor for the farm. By the 1960s I was an international press photographer working in Vietnam, Japan and particularly Africa. I was in Chad when my father died.

By this time Jean and his wife Lilette were running the farm. They had four daughters, who filled the farm with life again. They were all born after the new motorway had reduced the farm to half its size. My mother still lived there. When I talked to her on the telephone, she always asked me when I was going to come home. She died seven years after my father, aged seventy-eight.

Five years later, my brother sold his cattle. Now he's more of a market gardener than a farmer. He sells his produce to the Le Garet shopping centre which has been built on my father's old fields. You can see the McDonalds' sign from the farmyard. Apparently at night there are prostitutes. Yesterday Le Garet was the country, now it's the outskirts of the town. And tomorrow?

On days when the light is beautiful, when the sun is red above the Saône, I find myself regretting not having come more often when my parents were working the farm. Or having gone up to Paris to photograph Jean-Luc Godard and Jean Seberg on the release of *A Bout de Souffle*. There were more beautiful photographs to be taken here on this unremarkable farm: the peasants' work, ploughing, milking, the harvests. I don't want to turn this into an exercise in nostalgia, but I would love to have a good picture of my father. Perhaps these few prints are the best photographs I've taken. □

My parents' bedroom on the farm at Le Garet. My parents died long ago, but nothing has been changed. The portraits of their two children are still there, taken by the Claude studio in Villefranche-sur-Saône. My brother Jean is on the left, I am on the right.

Villefranche was the nearest town. Me in shorts and lace-up boots.

Our farmyard. One of the first images I developed myself.

Opposite: Mum and Sylvestre, our Polish farm labourer, under the stone staircase, next to the plane tree. The staircase is my first childhood memory. At first I was only allowed on the bottom steps and I'd look into the kitchen. Later I'd do acrobatics on the iron rail.

Bread and a few staples were brought by the grocer at Savigneux, Monsieur Messan, who used to come to the farmyard once a week. Everything else came from the garden or the farm. The farm workers ate their meals with us. Edouard put wine in his soup and my mother was fond of the summer supplement of the Lyon newspaper, *Le Progrès*.

Opposite top: Sylvestre in the fields. I liked him a lot. He was skilful and stubborn. He used to call me Champion. These fields have long since been turned into commercial and residential land.

Opposite bottom: My parents, the day their first tractor arrived, a grey Fergusson. It was a big local event! My father sold the oxen, but he didn't want to sell his horses or send them to the abattoir.

11 May 1958. My brother rides a friend's Vespa on the Beauregard road, just before he went to Morocco on military service, aged nineteen.

Sylvestre was often drunk on Sunday evening when he came home from his day off. We both loved Pernod the dog.

My first
photograph,
taken when I
was ten.

My first commission: to photograph the Perraud family children. Their mother,
Marie Perraud, used to come to the farm every evening to get fresh milk. She
suggested that I take photos of her seven children. My mother must have let her
know she was worried: 'He wants to be a photographer!'

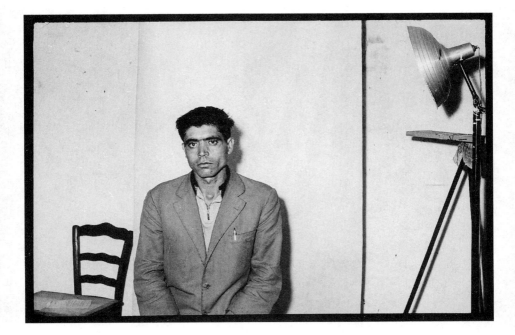

Opposite top: I needed a passport photo to get the 'Camera Buff,
Two Stars' card on my correspondence course.

Opposite bottom: An Italian farm worker.

Above: During the holidays I learnt to drive in this Renault Juva 4 on the little lanes
around the farm.

Opposite: After the A6 Paris–Lyon motorway was built in the 1960s, all the fields on the western side of my family's farm were decreed an industrial zone and compulsorily purchased. With the proceeds, my parents bought me a little flat on the sixth floor of a new building in rue Falguière, Paris.

My parents were happy when I came to see them in my car. My father was sixty; my brother and sister-in-law had decided to come and work on the farm at Le Garet. I was glad, the farm was saved.

Here I am with my niece Sylvie, probably photographed by Christine, her older sister.

Opposite: My father always dressed in blue, winter and summer. I often saw him getting changed during the day.

The television was popular with my little nieces.

Opposite page: 1975. Polaroid of my father with his daughter-in-law and grandchildren at the time of his illness. A specialist at Grange-Blanche hospital told my brother that my father's generation had been worn out by work. My father left school at twelve to take over from his father who was called up for the 1914 war.

My father died during my eight-month stay in Chad in 1975-76. I found out only when I got back. My brother and my mother came to Geneva to tell me. The fact of finding out so late troubled me for a long time. The light on the lake was so beautiful when I heard those terrible words. To take my mind off it, the Gamma agency sent me to the Olympic games in Montreal.

I put up a large map of Africa in the kitchen so my mother could follow my journeys.

With this Aaton camera, I made two ten-minute films about my mother. My little nieces got her to talk about who she was in love with as a young girl. The film has never been edited, it's somewhere in Paris in storage.

Sometimes when I came home I'd take my mother to this cemetery in Arnas where my father is buried.

Badminton in the farmyard at Le Garet. But does Le Garet exist
any more? My nieces prefer to say that they live in
Villefranche, just past the motorway, rue Blaise-Pascal.

Cultural Studies from Cambridge

Victorian Literature and Culture

Now published by Cambridge twice a year, Victorian Literature and Culture encourages high quality original work concerned with all areas of Victorian literature and culture, including music and the fine arts. The journal presents work at the cutting edge of current research, including exciting new studies in untouched subjects or new methodologies.

Subscriptions
Volume 19 in 1997: September
£66 for institutions; £35 for individuals; prices include delivery by air. ISSN 0144-7564.

●●●●●●●●●●●●●●●●●●●●●●●●●●●●●●●●●●

Prospects

Prospects is a multidisciplinary journal that explores all aspects of American civilisation. The journal publishes in interdisciplinary subject areas ranging over literature, film, humour, satire, photography, music, history, art, urban studies, television and sociology. Each volume is lavishly illustrated.

Subscriptions
Volume 22 in 1997: October;£53 for institutions; £30 for individuals; prices include delivery by air. ISSN 0361-2333.

Comparative Criticism

Comparative Criticism is an annual journal of comparative literature and cultural studies that has gained an international reputation since its inception in 1979. Aside from literary theory and criticism, it includes translations of literary, scholarly and critical works and substantial reviews of important books in the field.

Subscriptions
Volume 19 in 1997: September
£66 for institutions; £35 for individuals;; prices include delivery by air. ISSN 0144-7564.

●●●●●●●●●●●●●●●●●●●●●●●●●●●●●●●●●●

Journal of American Studies

Journal of American Studies publishes works by scholars from all over the world on American literature, history, institutions, politics, economics, film, popular culture, geography, sociology and related subjects. A 'Notes and Comments' section provides a forum for shorter pieces and responses from readers to points made in articles or reviews.

Subscriptions
Volume 31 in 1997: April, August and December: £69 for institutions. Prices include delivery by air. ISSN 0021-8758.

Further Information   52998

Please send me further information on _____

Name _____

Address _____

_____

Send coupon to Journals Marketing Department, Cambridge University Press, Publishing Division, Shaftesbury Road, Cambridge, CB2 3RU
Tel: +44(0)1223 325829 Fax: +44(0)1223 325959
E-mail: journals_marketing@cup.cam.ac.uk

CAMBRIDGE
UNIVERSITY PRESS

Edinburgh Building, Shaftebury Road, Cambridge

GRANTA

BRIAN CATHCART
THE CASE OF STEPHEN LAWRENCE

Stephen Lawrence was murdered on the night of 22 April 1993, in Eltham, a south-eastern suburb of London. He was on his way home with a friend, Duwayne Brooks. Both Lawrence and Brooks were eighteen years old and both were black. Lawrence was at school studying for his A levels; Brooks was at college learning electronics. It was a Thursday. Lawrence had been at school; Brooks had a day off college. They met at the gates of Lawrence's school, hung around in Lewisham for a while and then went to Mottingham, where they spent the evening at the home of Lawrence's uncle, eating dinner and playing Super Nintendo. At 9.55 p.m. they left the Mottingham house and began their complicated bus journey home. Stephen's parents did not like him to be out late.

Lawrence lived in Plumstead. Mottingham and Plumstead are only three miles apart, but the journey involved three buses on different routes; this part of London has never been penetrated by the Underground, and most main roads run east to west. Lawrence and Brooks were travelling south to north, parallel to the line of the primary meridian which cuts through Greenwich, a couple of miles to the west. The first bus took them to Eltham High Street and a second to a well-known local interchange, Well Hall Roundabout. There they walked fifty yards to a bus stop in Well Hall Road from which they could take a third bus the mile or so over the hill to Plumstead. They reached the stop at 10.25 p.m.

Three other people waited there with them: a young French au pair girl and two white men, one in his thirties and the other in his late teens. According to the later statements of these three people, Lawrence and Brooks passed the time chatting about football, and one of them practised a few dance steps.

Fifteen minutes passed. No bus came. The boys got restless. If at the beginning of these fifteen minutes they had decided to walk the rest of the way, they would have been almost home by now. Plumstead was only a mile and a quarter away. Brooks suggested a different route home, on a bus which used another exit from the roundabout, but Lawrence was reluctant to move; the other route was less direct. Brooks then walked a few yards back towards the roundabout to see if a bus was coming. He spotted one in the distance, and also a group of young white men on the far side of the roundabout moving their way. There were half a dozen of them. Brooks turned and moved towards Lawrence, calling: 'Can you see the bus?'

Lawrence didn't reply; perhaps he hadn't heard the question. Brooks called again: 'Can you see it?'

The time was 10.40 p.m.

The white boys were by now just across the road and within earshot. One called out: 'What, what, nigger?'

Then the white group started to run across the road towards Lawrence and Brooks. Brooks ran from them, yelling to Lawrence to run too. But Lawrence didn't, perhaps because he hadn't quite understood what Brooks was warning him of. The white group surrounded him, punching and kicking him and pulling him to the ground. One of the white boys chased Brooks briefly and then turned back to join in the beating of Lawrence.

It was over in a few seconds. The white boys ran off down a residential side street, Dickson Road. Lawrence got to his feet and ran in the other direction, across Well Hall Road. His friend rejoined him. 'Duwayne,' said Lawrence. 'Just run,' said Brooks.

They covered about a hundred yards. Brooks was ahead when he heard Lawrence call again.

'Look at me, tell me what's wrong.'

Brooks turned and saw blood pumping through Lawrence's jacket.

'Just keep running,' he said.

'I can't, I can't,' Lawrence said. Then he collapsed.

Brooks saw a phone box, ran to it, and dialled 999, asking for an ambulance. The operator seemed uncertain of the phone box's location. Brooks wasn't sure that he had been understood. He left the phone off the hook and ran out into the traffic on Well Hall Road, trying to flag down passing cars; none stopped. He asked a couple of pedestrians for help; they walked on. He tried the telephone again, and again there was confusion—panicky incoherence at one end, perhaps, and incomprehension at the other.

A car stopped; the driver was an off-duty policeman. Lawrence had lost consciousness by now and Brooks was agitated and distressed. He told the policeman that he'd called for an ambulance but that the woman at the other end hadn't listened to

The Lawrences meet Nelson Mandela

TIDDY MAITLAND-TITTERTON

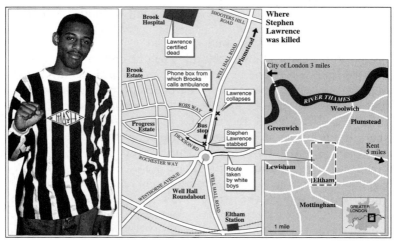

Brook
Hospital

SHOOTERS HILL
ROAD

Lawrence
certified
dead

Brook
Estate

Phone box from
which Brooks
calls ambulance

ROSS WAY

WELL HALL ROAD

Plumstead

Lawrence
collapses

Progress
Estate

Bus
stop

DICKSON RD

Stephen
Lawrence
stabbed

ROCHESTER WAY

WESTHORNE AVENUE

Well Hall
Roundabout

Route
taken
by white
boys

WELL HALL ROAD

Eltham
Station

1 mile

**Where
Stephen
Lawrence
was killed**

City of London 3 miles

RIVER THAMES

Woolwich

Greenwich

Plumstead

Kent
5 miles

Lewisham

Eltham

Mottingham

GREATER
LONDON

MICHAEL ROSCOE

him. The policeman went to the phone and came back to say that an ambulance was on its way. A couple came out of a church nearby. The woman knelt beside Lawrence and realized she could do nothing but comfort him and pray. She thought he seemed peaceful. Two uniformed police officers, a man and a woman, arrived next. Brooks asked: 'Where's the fucking ambulance? I didn't call the police.' He urged the policeman to take Stephen to hospital by car. According to Brooks: 'He said he couldn't. He said he was going to handcuff me because I was getting hysterical.'

An ambulance arrived at 10.54 p.m., but Lawrence was no longer breathing and his heart had stopped beating. He was taken to Brook Hospital, a mile away. At 11.17 p.m. he was certified dead.

The autopsy showed that he had been stabbed twice with a large knife, once in the shoulder and once close to the collarbone. The blows were probably struck while he was still standing and entered the body in a downward direction, severing vital arteries and veins. Lawrence bled to death from these blows, but the attack had been so quick and so confusing that the three people at the bus stop, watching from only twenty-five yards away, thought they had witnessed a scuffle rather than a stabbing. None of them had seen a weapon; they saw only that Stephen had been pulled to the ground and kicked. When he got to his feet and ran, it looked as though he was not badly hurt. All three boarded the bus when it came along, but one of them, the white teenager, Joe Shepherd, recognized Lawrence as a boy from his neighbourhood. When he got home, he told his father. Father and son then went to tell Stephen's parents, Neville and Doreen Lawrence, that they thought Stephen might have been badly beaten. In search of their son, the Lawrences drove first to the bus stop and then to the hospital, where, after a short wait, they were told that he had died.

These are the principal events in the murder of Stephen Lawrence, so far as they are known. There is little about them to suggest that he would become the most famous black victim of murder in British history.

2

Stephen Lawrence's parents were migrants from Jamaica. Neville Lawrence came to Britain in search of work in 1960, when he was eighteen. Doreen came at around the same time as the ten-year-old daughter of a large immigrant family. Neville worked as a plasterer and decorator; Doreen, after five or six years at school, as a clerk in the National Westminster Bank. They met at a concert in 1972 and married in the same year. Stephen, their first child, was born in 1974 and was followed by another son, Stuart, and a daughter, Georgina. By this time the Lawrences had settled in Plumstead, in an estate of council houses dominated by a tower block. This, the Nightingale Estate, named possibly after the nurse or possibly after the songbird, is the kind of place that exemplifies the limitations (and excesses) of British municipal planning in the 1960s, but the Lawrences rented a house on the edge of the estate in one of its pleasanter streets. They did well. They worked, they saved, they went to church. Eventually, they bought their house. By 1993, they had enjoyed their average share of British fortune and misfortune. The recession in the building trade in the early 1990s had put Neville Lawrence out of work for a year. Doreen Lawrence, on the other hand, had gone back to work after ten years at home looking after her children. She had progressed from serving school dinners to looking after children with special educational needs. Her colleagues recognized her gifts and her intelligence and encouraged her to get the qualifications that would allow her promotion. In 1992 she began her first year of a humanities course at what is now the University of Greenwich.

The Lawrences believed in good behaviour and they were, by modern standards, strict with their children. They wanted them to get on. The children grew up to be bright and well behaved; Stephen, since his death, has often been described as a 'model teenager'. He had been a cub and a scout, he studied hard (homework came before television) and had ambitions to qualify as an architect. Besides school and the friendships formed there, his world was mostly an extension of his parents' world, which was defined by three communities: the extended family, and especially Doreen's relatives; the local Methodist church; and the family's neighbours on the Nightingale Estate. The first was black, the second a mixture of black and white, the third mainly white. But that was to see things racially, and the Lawrences were neither defensive nor assertive about their race. They got on with their white fellow churchgoers and particularly well with their white next-door neighbours, who had children of similar ages. They could be (and were later to be) portrayed as an example of typical British family life, even though this respectable model was dwindling everywhere, among all classes and races: the Christian, undivorced, two-parent family who wanted the best for their children. Because of these virtues, they could be set against a notion of black life in Britain popular among white people: typified by lone teenage mothers, educational under-achievement, unemployment and criminality. And so, depending through which stereotypical prism they were viewed, they were an unremarkable family in one way and a remarkable one in another.

But perhaps their most remarkable quality was this: that they had sustained their belief in the fairness of British society against a political tide which among non-white communities ran generally in the opposite direction, and they had sustained it while living in the London borough of Greenwich.

The world knows Greenwich for its meridian, its mean time, its naval college and museum, its royal palace and its historic observatory. It grew up as a maritime outpost of London, supplying the Royal Navy with ships, guns, sailors, charts and victuals. Fine Georgian terraces climb up among its parkland. Beyond them, over the horizon that is available from the river, lies a Greenwich which the world knows less about, the residential hinterland: Plumstead, Eltham and Mottingham. These suburbs are neither bad nor mean, nor even lacking a history of their own. The medieval kings of England spent their summers in a palace in Eltham. Bob Hope was born in Eltham; W. G. Grace, the most celebrated cricketer of all time, lived in Eltham. Until late in the last century most of it was fields; early in this century it became a refuge for the self-improver, the upwardly mobile working-class who were quitting inner London for houses with gardens that offered easier access to the countryside of Kent, 'the garden of

England'. Stand at the spot where Stephen Lawrence waited for his bus, where Dickson Road joins Well Hall Road, and you can see the unmistakable stamp of the architects and planners of the 'Garden City' movement and the brand of idealism which tried to bring rural England, Olde England, to the town. The houses have steep roofs and dainty windows—the English cottage was their inspiration—and stand well back behind trees, wide lawns and hedges. Dickson Road twists down westward into a jumble of gardened streets. It is supposed to feel like a village; and it does.

It is called the Progress Estate, and it was built during the First World War to house the thousands of munitions workers who had been recruited by the Woolwich Arsenal and who took the tram along Well Hall Road each morning to make shells and bombs. The trams went long ago, and then the arsenal closed along with many other riverside factories; the story of work in Eltham over the past thirty years is common to the western world. Employment, especially for young males, can be difficult to find. But the Progress Estate—perhaps unlike some of the people who live on it—has not been much damaged by this transformation. Architecture students come to admire it. And, partly because the local authority which once owned the houses obeyed the wishes of the inhabitants that the estate should house their kith and kin, it is still nearly one hundred per cent white.

The white boys who killed Lawrence ran down Dickson Road. Were they running home?

3

Here is a joke that was popular in Eltham around the time of the murder: Question: 'How long does it take a nigger to shit?' Answer: 'Nine months.' And here is some popular Eltham world history: 'My aunt said AIDS only got over in this country 'cos a black man fucked a monkey, right, and then he fucked a white person, and then . . . ' Both of these were collected in the year after Lawrence's death by a group of researchers led by Roger Hewitt of the Institute for Education at the University of London. Hewitt went to Eltham to look for racism. His surprise was not that he found it—in 1996, police in the borough of Greenwich recorded 440 incidents of racial harassment, one of the highest numbers, district by district, in the United Kingdom—but that it seemed almost eager to be found. In his paper, 'Routes of Racism', Hewitt wrote: 'In some neighbourhoods it seemed that open and unapologetic racism was wall to wall amongst adolescents, with almost no gaps.'

Hewitt and his team found that this hostility to non-whites (of Asian as well as African-Caribbean descent) was not a birthright—it had not been learned from parents, handed down from a more bigoted time. Instead, it had been generated and sustained by the young. Hewitt wrote: 'The racism of adolescents was a world of its own, policed from within through criticism of anyone who flirted with interracial friendships, and of those "wiggers"—"white niggers"—who came near to embracing black youth culture.' Many white children encountered black people of their own age only when they reached secondary school at the age of eleven or twelve. The schools asked them to conform to strict anti-racist policies. Many came to feel, according to Hewitt, that 'too much attention' was paid to the problems of black people, that black people were protected by special rules, that 'ethnic minority' cultures were taken more seriously than theirs, or even that they had no culture of their own. One boy complained: 'Say you 'ave a fight with a black person, I reckon the school itself is racist towards white people. Like, you see, they always take up a black kid's side and they don't wanna know what your version of the story is.'

In many areas of London—of Britain—non-whites form a far larger percentage of the population than in Eltham. In Greenwich as a whole their proportion is only thirteen per cent. But manifestations of racial hatred do not rise in unerring proportion to the number of non-whites in any given area—the more blacks, the more acts of hostility and harassment from whites. The opposite may be the case. According to Roger Hewitt, it wasn't an accident that many white youths in Eltham spoke and behaved as they did. Eltham was predominantly white, but it bordered, to the west, on the more racially mixed areas of inner London and, to the east, on the middle-class white suburbia of Kent. A white

153

Dickson Road, Eltham; a suburban version of village England.
Lawrence was stabbed near to where the woman is walking.

TOM PILSTON

youth in Eltham could see himself or herself holding a front line: they shall not pass. 'People who move [in] round here that are black, they get knocked off this estate 'cos they don't like 'em,' one girl told Hewitt's group. Her friend added: 'And they go. They can't put up wiv no more so they 'ave to go.'

A nearly literate scrawl on a church gate declared: WATCH OUT COONS, YOUR NOW ENTERING ELTHAM.

4

The police summoned a press conference the day after Lawrence died. His father appeared and said: 'I would bring back hanging for something like this.' His mother was under sedation. The headmaster of Lawrence's school said he was a very popular pupil and 'not the sort to get himself into trouble'. Duwayne Brooks, meanwhile, had spent much of the night and the following morning giving a long statement to the police. It included the words he'd heard near the roundabout—'What, what, nigger?'—and on this basis the police acknowledged that Lawrence had probably been killed because he was black, that it was a murder motivated purely by race. Chief Superintendent John Philpott spoke of fears of a backlash among the black community. 'We would ask young people to be sensible,' he said. Extra police were drafted in, not to investigate the murder, but to keep the peace.

Many blacks and Asians in Eltham were angry, and directed their anger towards the police. Lawrence's killing was the third (by some counts the fourth) racial murder in the borough of Greenwich over the previous two years, and the second to have occurred on Well Hall Road. A phrase appeared in some newspaper reports—'the racist murder capital of Britain'—though the story at this stage was not front-page news in the press, nor was it reported on national television news bulletins. The Metropolitan Police, which has very few non-white recruits, was accused of failing to protect the minority community. A particular focus of anger was the headquarters of the anti-black, anti-immigrant British National Party on Welling Road, just three or four miles from Eltham. A BNP spokesman denied any link to the killing, but anti-racist activists announced their plans for demonstrations outside the party's office.

Over the next few weeks there were several such demonstrations. One of them ended in violence between demonstrators and the police.

The relationship between the police and the Lawrence family began to break down. The Lawrences had lived in the middle of racial harassment for many years without being politicized by it. They had never personally experienced abuse or violence, had no idea why so many black people were critical of the police, and disapproved of anti-police views. Neville Lawrence told a reporter at this time: 'We'd hear about these racial things happening, but we'd think it would never happen to us. We tried to bring up our kids in the right way, to obey the law.' It was in that spirit that he agreed to appear at the police press conference, where he made his remark about hanging.

Nevertheless, the police began to blame the influence of 'outsiders'. Two weeks after Stephen's death the *Daily Mail* published a piece about the case under the headline: HOW RACE MILITANTS HIJACKED A TRAGEDY. It said that radical anti-racist organizations were exploiting the killing for their own political ends and damaging the trust between the Lawrences and the police that was vital if the killers were to be identified and arrested. An anonymous police officer was quoted: 'At the beginning we were very close to the family and had a good rapport. But later we had to go through several representatives before we could speak to them . . . We believe that the family are being used as pawns in a far wider game. Our inquiries are, in fact, being hampered by these people.'

The police were to make this claim many times. How true was it? Undeniably, many non-whites in Greenwich felt antagonism towards the police and there were vociferous radical groups articulating those feelings. Some of them made approaches to the Lawrence family and for a time one group did work closely with them: the Anti-Racist Alliance (ARA), led by a television journalist, Marc Wadsworth. But the ARA could hardly be painted as extremist. Several Labour Members of Parliament supported it and its members included a range of people to whom the word 'liberal' might apply. ARA members began work at the Lawrence house in Plumstead on the morning after Stephen's murder, answering calls, taking the other two children to school, helping to deal with the press and the police.

Three days after the murder the Lawrences also hired a solicitor to represent them, Imran Khan, who could certainly be described as radical (in the 1997 general election he stood as a candidate for Arthur Scargill's Socialist Labour Party). But he was also well known to be good at handling racial cases. From the day he was hired he was almost always present when the Lawrences met police officers. The police didn't like it. Few of them had encountered a victim's family which turned up with a lawyer, except in cases where the family was suspected of involvement.

Were the Lawrences used as pawns by Khan or Wadsworth? Naturally, both men have denied it; Wadsworth said frankly that the Lawrences wouldn't give him the control he wanted, preferring to trust their own judgements or the advice of relatives. Ros Howells, a social worker and a friend of Doreen's who attended many meetings between the Lawrences and the police, confirmed this: 'When you know Doreen Lawrence, you know that she is not led by anyone.' In other words, the Lawrences make unlikely pawns; and even if they had been pawns, it is hard to see how Khan or Wadsworth could have interfered with any halfway competent murder investigation. Unless, of course, the family were suspects.

Were they suspects? Surely not; the police had the evidence of Duwayne Brooks and Joe Shepherd, the boy waiting at the bus stop, which pointed them clearly towards a white gang. The Lawrences, however, *felt* like suspects. They may have felt like this whatever their race. In about eighty per cent of British murder cases, the murderer is close to the victim in some way—husband, wife, uncle, cousin, friend—and the methods of police investigation reflect this statistic. Like many other relatives of murder victims, the Lawrences felt that they were being treated with too little sympathy and being given too little information.

They were angered in particular by the persistent scrutiny of their own lives. To the Lawrences the cause of the murder was simple; why could the police not concentrate on finding the boys who did it? Instead—or so it seemed to the Lawrences—the police went on questioning them, the family who had suffered. Three days after his son's death, Neville Lawrence was upset to find the police pressing him to explain why Stephen had been wearing a brightly coloured baseball cap. Was it a piece of gang insignia?

The Lawrences began to feel that the reason for this persistence was their race. As Doreen Lawrence said later: 'They'd never come across a black boy who didn't have a criminal record. They couldn't believe it. And when they finally did, they decided he must have been part of a gang and his death must have been connected to a fight between rival gangs. For two weeks they concentrated their investigation on us and what we'd done wrong.'

The Lawrences also felt that the murder of their son had not received the media attention that many people, including the then Conservative MP for Eltham, Peter Bottomley, felt that it deserved. An appalling murder, which is what it was, had been muted by the victim's colour, so that it became a racial 'incident'. The police effort to find the killers seemed to lack energy. So far as the Lawrences could tell, the police had not carried out systematic house-to-house inquiries in the Progress Estate or Dickson Road on the night of the killing. No one had been taken in for questioning, even though, over the following days, callers at the Lawrence home supplied a number of names of people thought to have been involved. The effect, say the family, was that any opportunity of capturing the killers in the process of disposing of clothing or weapons was lost. Instead, the extra police who arrived at the scene on the night, and who might have carried out some of this work, were sent away again. Fourteen days passed before the first arrests, by which time the forensic trail had gone cold. To the Lawrences, it seemed that the best chance of convicting their son's killers was thrown away before he had been dead a week.

On 4 May, the Lawrences gave a press conference to vent their anger. 'Nothing has been done,' Doreen Lawrence said. 'There have been no arrests and the police won't tell us what's happening. The black community and I cannot stand for this any longer. The killers are out there and other black kids can't feel safe on the streets.' Her husband added: 'The police are not really concerned about arresting anyone. They are just going through the motions.' (Much later, Doreen Lawrence would describe an incident at this time which particularly shocked her. She took to the police station a list of the names of her son's alleged killers provided by friends and sympathizers. 'I presented it to one of the officers and while we were talking I watched. He folded the paper and rolled it into a ball in his hand. I asked "Are you going to throw it in the bin?" He said "No, no."' In fact, two of the six names on the list figured in later legal proceedings.)

Two days later the police met the Lawrences to try to clear the air. They insisted that they were pursuing the case vigorously, with twenty-five officers working full-time from the incident room at Plumstead police station, and they invited the Lawrences to visit the station to see the work in progress. (The invitation was refused.) The police also said that they were properly investigating the many tip-offs they had received. The officers left the meeting believing that a 'fragile peace' had been established.

They were wrong. The next day the Lawrences staged a remarkable publicity coup. Nelson Mandela, on only his second visit to Britain since his release from jail, agreed to meet them. The Lawrences emerged from Mandela's hotel in central London to face a crowd of reporters and camera crews. They complained about the 'cavalier' attitude of the police and the police's failure to act on the information they had been given. Their complaints were widely reported. Two weeks after the murder, the Lawrence case had at last become news.

5

Perhaps coincidentally, the police made their first arrests the same day. Since the start of their investigation, they had been given many tip-offs, both from their regular professional informers and from the ordinary residents of Eltham. One anonymous telephone caller told them that they would find a knife in a dustbin behind the Welcome Inn on Well Hall Road. The policeman who went found nothing in the bin, but got back to his car to find a piece of paper stuck to the rear window. The paper listed four names of the five who were later arrested. (Later a senior police officer, answering criticism about the slowness of the Lawrence investigation, said this tip-off alone 'was insufficient to warrant an arrest, but we took immediate action on it. It was thoroughly researched and we mounted a full surveillance operation.')

On 7 May, the day of the Mandela meeting, the police arrested Neil and Jamie Acourt and Gary Dobson. On 10 May, they arrested David Norris. On 3 June, they arrested Luke Knight. All five were members of a well-known local gang.

Neil and Jamie Acourt, then aged seventeen and sixteen, were brothers and the gang's leading figures. They lived five or ten minutes' walk from the scene of the killing in the Brook Estate, which lacks the charms of its neighbour, the Progress Estate, but is smart enough. The houses are solid and pre-war and built mostly of warm, dark brick, with plenty of gardens and open space. The Acourt home was one of the shabbiest on the estate; the parents had split up and Neil and Jamie shared the house with two older twin brothers and some pit bull terriers. They were known around the Brook as rough boys, and this seems to have pleased them. They liked to be known, after east London's most famous criminal family, as 'the Krays'.

Both had been in trouble before. Neil was alleged to have attacked a black player in a visiting team during a football match at a local sports club, and he and Jamie were thrown out of a youth club when they were caught painting 'NF' (for National Front) in letters three feet high on the wall. They had also persistently harassed one Asian family who had bought a council house on the estate; the council's solution was to buy the house back and move the family elsewhere. Once, in school, Jamie Acourt had threatened another boy with a revolver. He had also been cautioned by police for carrying knives. It was quite common on the Brook Estate for boys to carry weapons, but Neil and Jamie Acourt were particular offenders. When the police arrested them for the Lawrence killing, they found in the Acourt home a revolver, a shoulder holster, six knives including a Gurkha knife, and a sword in its scabbard. The Gurkha knife had been hidden under a bed, as had the revolver.

Gary Dobson, seventeen, lived in the Progress Estate, just two or three minutes from the scene of the killing. He was slower, softer and plumper than the hard-edged Acourts. The group sometimes treated him as a bit of a dimwit. When the police asked him to account for his movements on the night of 22 April, he said he had been at home all night, but soon changed his story to say he had called on the Acourts just before midnight to borrow some CDs. At the time of his arrest, police removed from his home a jacket which matched in some respects Duwayne Brooks's description of the jacket worn by one of Lawrence's attackers. They also confiscated two knives and a CS gas canister.

Luke Knight, sixteen, was the quietest and youngest member of the group. He was said to be related to Ronnie Knight, the Great Train Robber, and lived with his parents in a house close to Well Hall Roundabout. When arrested he claimed, like Dobson, to have been at home all evening on the night of the killing. He also said that he did not associate with the other boys, which was later demonstrated to be untrue.

David Norris, seventeen, lived to the south of Eltham in a more comfortable and middle-class area than the Brook or the Progress estates. His father, Clifford, was a well-known south London criminal who had been jailed for gun and drugs offences after several Kalashnikov rifles were found in the family home. A folding knife was taken from David Norris's house at the time of his arrest.

There can hardly have been anyone on the Brook and Progress estates who did not know this group. None of them had found a regular job since leaving school and they spent a lot of their time on the streets and in local pubs and clubs. People, and especially black and Asian people, knew not to cross them. As a senior police officer said later, the Acourt gang was 'a well-known and feared group in the community'.

Jamie Acourt and David Norris had already been charged with a knife attack the year before on a white youth in Chislehurst, a few miles away. That case was dropped. Now at least two more stabbings in Eltham in the two months before Lawrence's death were being looked into by the police.

Information about these crimes and the subsequent inquiries into them is scant, but they have certain elements in common. They were casual stabbings carried out by young white males and witnesses were so few that only a fragmentary picture of what occurred ever emerged; even the victims were reluctant to account for their wounds.

The police had made little or no headway in these cases at the time of the Stephen Lawrence killing, but after the Acourt boys and Norris were arrested they were interviewed about some of these other crimes and took part in identity parades related to them, so that several investigations involving the same suspects were under way at the same time. Charges were laid in one case against Neil Acourt and Norris, but they never came to court.

6

The key witness was Duwayne Brooks. But the weeks that followed his friend's murder were exceptionally hard for him. The two boys had been close for years, but Brooks was not a favourite with Stephen's parents; he was too streetwise, too 'raggamuffin'. For Brooks, however, Stephen's friendship was very important. He'd been unsettled since leaving school at sixteen and had found it hard to adjust to his college course. Stephen Lawrence was one of the few constants in his life and the murder overwhelmed him; he had survived and Stephen hadn't. Should he have run? Could he have staunched the bleeding? Could he have saved Stephen somehow? Anyone would ask themselves these questions.

Brooks's long statement to the police and his potential as an identification witness were to prove central to all efforts to bring the killers to justice, for in the years that have followed no one else has come forward to identify the perpetrators with confidence. It was a large burden for a traumatized eighteen-year-old to carry on behalf of the Lawrence family. Neither he nor they found it easy to face each other and he never joined what became the family's campaign. Instead, he became caught up in what one lawyer called 'a sequence of truly extraordinary events'.

On Saturday 8 May, the day after the first arrests, Duwayne

joined a protest march to the British National Party office in Welling Road which was organized by a group called Youth Against Racism. A few thousand took part, and it ended in violence. Bricks and bottles were thrown at the police, a car was overturned, and by some accounts shops were looted. About twenty people were hurt. It would subsequently be alleged that Duwayne Brooks played a part in this violence.

In May and June, Brooks was taking part in three identification parades, picking out Neil Acourt and Luke Knight, but not Gary Dobson. On the day he identified Knight, Brooks was given a lift home by a police sergeant, who later made a formal statement about a conversation which he said took place in the car. Duwayne allegedly asked if he had picked out the right person, saying that he had heard the Acourt brothers were responsible for the murder and that he thought the person he had identified was Jamie Acourt (it was not). This was innocuous enough, although lawyers for the Lawrence family believe it would have been the proper procedure for the sergeant to have stopped the conversation at that point. According to the sergeant's statement, however, Brooks went on to make two important comments. First, that he couldn't remember the faces of any of Stephen's killers, only their general appearances; second, that he suspected that he had picked out the right person from the line-up because the man looked as though he had spent the previous night in the cells.

Brooks later denied saying anything beyond asking if he had picked out the right person, and lawyers for the Lawrence family have raised a number of questions about the alleged conversation and the way it was reported, which they regard as highly unusual. But it could make no difference: a powerful weapon had been placed in the hands of the defence in any future prosecution. Brooks's anger and distress on the night and his rudeness towards the police were already obvious as strategies available to cast doubt on his testimony. Now there was the added evidence of a police sergeant to suggest that his identifications were unsound.

During these weeks, Brooks twice spotted young men whom he believed had been among Lawrence's assailants. Once, when he was with a journalist in a pub in Lewisham, he thought he saw the

Duwayne Brooks

person who had actually stabbed Stephen. Then, outside a fast-food restaurant in Greenwich, he thought he recognized another of the gang, who looked like the brother of one of the men he had identified in a parade. These random sightings shocked Brooks, and they later brought confusion to his testimony.

Other witnesses came forward with fragments of evidence, including sightings of young men running down streets which led to the Brook Estate, where the Acourts lived. There was also the evidence of the many knives and other weapons found at the suspects' homes. Dobson and Knight, moreover, had both lied to police during questioning and given questionable alibis. One of the most colourful pieces of evidence was an entry in the diary of a local girl, Michelle Casserley, who knew the suspects well. A few days after the murder, she wrote: *'Acourts stabbed a black boy up Well Hall Road. Jamie, Neil, Gary, David and Lukey.'* This was all useful, but it was nowhere near as important as Brooks's word.

The police thought they had a case and forwarded their papers to the Crown Prosecution Service (CPS), which conducts every criminal prosecution by the state in England and Wales, about 1.5 million cases a year. The CPS has discretion over which cases it will pursue, and its guidelines state that a prosecution should be in the public interest and should have at least a fifty-fifty chance of leading to conviction. Both are subjective measures, and in 1993 the service was criticized by pressure groups and politicians for the way it applied them. It was said that the CPS was too keen to keep its conviction rate high, and therefore too ready to drop what in its view were the more marginal cases, or to reduce charges against defendants in order to avoid defeats. As a result, it was said, many criminals were going unpunished.

A date for the committal hearing—the preliminary to a full trial before a judge and jury—was set and the body of Stephen Lawrence was released to his parents after a second post-mortem, which had been ordered by defence lawyers. At last the Lawrences could set about burying their son. A memorial service was held at Trinity Methodist Church in Plumstead attended by, among others, the local MP, Peter Bottomley, and two black Labour MPs, Paul Boateng and Diane Abbott. The minister, who was a friend of the Lawrences, said: 'Many of us feel ashamed to be white.' Then the Lawrences flew with their son's body to Jamaica and on 4 July buried him in a grave next to his grandmother. They could not, by this stage, bear to think of him in a British grave and were beginning to think that, after the trial was over, they might restart their lives by leaving London for good and resettling in Jamaica.

They were still on the island when, on 29 July, the Crown Prosecution Service announced that the committal hearing, which was scheduled to begin the next day, would not go ahead. It was dropping the charges: 'after careful consideration of the available evidence in this case, we have decided that there is insufficient evidence to provide a realistic prospect of a conviction. We understand the police investigation is continuing and we will look at it again if more evidence is passed to us.' The five boys were discharged. The Lawrences were appalled and the police disappointed. Editorials in the broadsheet press criticized the CPS's judgement, arguing that this was further evidence of the service's excessive caution. Two MPs, Peter Bottomley and Paul Boateng, demanded explanations from the Attorney-General. Black groups were furious; the ARA spoke of 'something rotten at the heart of the Crown Prosecution Service'. But the service itself did not think, and has never thought since, that it made a mistake. It argues that the case was not dropped, but rather that a premature prosecution was prevented. Had it gone ahead, unsuccessfully, the five accused would have been immune from further action: you cannot face the same charge twice. The way had been kept open for the police to search for more and better evidence. This was not how the Lawrences and their supporters saw it at the time. In the absence of Stephen's parents, Imran Khan, the family solicitor, and Cheryl Sloley, Stephen's aunt, did the talking. 'It is quite unbelievable that the police have been unable to secure the evidence required to secure these youths for trial after three months,' said Khan. 'What we need now is a full explanation from the police as to what kind of investigation they carried out.' Cheryl Sloley was more bitter: 'We were constantly told by the police to trust them and that they were doing all they could. It obviously wasn't enough. As Nelson Mandela told us, black lives are cheap.'

7

Between August 1993, after the CPS decision, and April 1995, the second anniversary of Lawrence's death, the roles taken by family and police changed dramatically. The Lawrences, who had begun as helpless victims, became the prosecutors, taking responsibility themselves for the pursuit of justice. The police, who had been so much at odds with the family, gradually came to support them, seeking and supplying evidence to help the Lawrences, and giving advice. It became a partnership unique in British criminal history, though because of their previous antagonisms the relationship was never easy.

The police reassessed their evidence. Witnesses were re-questioned; a reward was offered for information; public appeals were made and thousands of leaflets were distributed. The same officer, Detective Superintendent Brian Weeden, remained in charge, but the inquiry was subjected to review by at least one officer from another part of the Metropolitan Police. Some new evidence began to turn up. A man who knew Neil Acourt and his friends came forward in November to say he had seen some of them running from the scene on the night of the killing. This man had been questioned in house-to-house inquiries after the murder and said then that he had seen nothing, but he came forward now, he said, because friends had persuaded him that he should. He insisted, however, that he would only testify if he was guaranteed anonymity. He became known as Witness B.

At around the same time Beryl Cullen, the mother of Gaynor Cullen, Gary Dobson's girlfriend, gave the police a long-bladed knife. She said that in March, before the murder, she had found this knife under her daughter's mattress and had hidden it in her kitchen, where she believed it had stayed until July. Under police questioning, Gary Dobson would later admit that the knife was his, but he told a quite different story about it, leaving open the possibility that he might have had it in April and hidden it in his girlfriend's house after the murder. The knife, experts determined, could have been the one that killed Stephen.

Meanwhile the inquest on Lawrence's death had still to be

held. Inquests exist simply to establish the cause of death—they are not a forum for prosecution—but the Lawrences wanted to use their son's to get the facts of the case before a jury, the media and the public. Michael Mansfield, the prominent left-wing barrister and Queen's Counsel, who had worked before with the solicitor, Imran Khan, would appear for the family; his presence in itself would raise the inquest's public profile. The inquest was barely under way, however, when Mansfield announced that 'dramatic' new evidence had been discovered. He asked for, and was granted, an indefinite adjournment. Through Greenwich Council, a report had come of a conversation in which one of the suspects was said to have confessed to the killing. The story was soon found to be untrue, but the inquest, adjourned late in 1993, did not resume for more than three years.

The renewed police investigation was completed early in 1994 and the file of evidence passed again to the Crown Prosecution Service, which again rejected the case. On 15 April 1994, it said: 'Despite the police's painstaking and thorough investigation, we concluded that on the basis of the information available there is insufficient evidence to take action against any individual.'

Once again there was outrage in the press, in the black community and among some politicians. The CPS was accused of stubbornly preventing the evidence from going before a jury, who by rights should be the people to weigh the evidence. The white legal system was condemned for failing black people. The Lawrences now had only one way forward, and they took it. Within a week they announced that they were considering a private prosecution against the five suspects, that the family itself would do what the CPS had refused to do, and take the five to court.

This was a bold course, and few lawyers would have regarded it as a practical one. Private prosecutions of any kind are rare—about one in 400 cases in England and Wales—and often fail. The experience of those who bring them suggests that they are at best tolerated and at worst obstructed by the legal authorities, and they can be ruinously expensive. As for a private prosecution for murder, the Lawrences' would be only the fourth in 130 years. If the CPS was convinced that on the available evidence success was unlikely, why did the family and its lawyers think otherwise? They had good reasons. They believed that there was reliable evidence on which a jury could convict, if only a jury could be allowed to hear it. They believed that more evidence might emerge in court, particularly if the defendants testified—Mansfield is a brilliant cross-examiner.

At a meeting with Sir Paul Condon, the Commissioner of the Metropolitan Police, the family had indicated that unless there were signs of a strong new official initiative, they would proceed alone. No new initiative came and the Lawrences announced their decision. The police saw that they had no choice but to help. The case had become a serious embarrassment to them and, to some extent, the government. It was now, for many people, a symbol both of racism and legal inadequacy. A conviction here, it was particularly clear to the police, would do more for the standing of the force than five convictions in less controversial cases.

Money and manpower poured into a new, third investigation, and Eltham police station became the setting for one of London's largest murder inquiries. Detective Superintendent Weeden retired—the Lawrences had always resented him—and Detective Superintendent Bill Mellish took charge. Mellish had just completed a long and racially sensitive re-investigation in north London into the events surrounding the murder of PC Keith Blakelock in the Broadwater Farm riots of 1985. He brought his team with him; there were now a dozen officers working full-time on the Lawrence case rather than four, and it is widely acknowledged, even by the Lawrences, that over the next year the police did all that they could to find evidence which could secure a conviction.

On 22 April 1995, the second anniversary of Stephen's death, the Lawrence family lawyers lodged an application before Greenwich magistrates for the issue of arrest warrants in a private prosecution for murder. Neil Acourt, Luke Knight and David Norris had been under surveillance and were seized within the hour. Knight told police: 'This is a fucking joke. I have been arrested for murder and I wasn't even there.' Jamie Acourt was also charged, but he was already in custody at Feltham Young Offenders' Institution in west London, awaiting trial for the attempted murder of a black youth in a Greenwich nightclub in August 1994. The fifth man, Gary Dobson, was charged later. On the same day as the arrests, the police handed to the Lawrences' lawyers all the evidence at their disposal: 4,500 pages of documentation and—an extraordinary and unexpected item—videotapes of four of the five accused relaxing at home with some friends.

8

The recordings had been made covertly over two weeks in December 1994, in a flat which Gary Dobson rented in Eltham and which the group (apart from Jamie Acourt, who was in custody) used as a base. Police had fitted a tiny microphone and camera to a power socket near the television, and it recorded a couple of dozen scenes in the private life of the Acourt group. Nowhere on the tapes are they captured confessing to the Lawrence murder—on the contrary, they deny involvement—but it is clear from the tapes that they suspected that they were being bugged, though unaware that they were also being filmed. Neil Acourt says at one point: 'I bet this gaff's bugged up to the eyebrows, mate.'

Here are Luke Knight and Neil Acourt discussing an international soccer game that they have been watching on television.

Knight complains about the commentary:

Luke Knight: . . . I think it was Cameroon, a fucking nigger country.

Neil Acourt: Who was saying that?

LK: Fucking our presenter. English presenters saying, 'Oh, yeah, we want Cameroon to win this.' Why the fuck should he want niggers to win it when they're playing, like, Italy or something, like a European fucking football team?

NA: It makes you sick dunnit?

LK: Gets on ya nerves.

NA [to television]: You rubber-lipped cunt. [Laughs] I reckon that every nigger should be chopped up, mate, and they should be left with nothing but fucking stumps.

LK: D'you remember that Enoch Powell? That geezer, he knew straight away. He went over to Africa and all that, right?

NA: Is that what happened?

LK: Yeah, he knew it was a slum. He knew it was a shithole and he came back here saying they're uncivilized and all that and then they started coming over here and he knew, he knew straight away. He was saying, 'No, I don't want them here. No fucking niggers; they'll ruin the gaff.' And he was right, they fucking have ruined it.

NA: Is he still alive?

LK: I seen him on a programme the other day.

NA: What was he saying?

LK: He wasn't saying nothing about niggers and all that, he was just saying about . . . something else.

NA: I wanna write him a letter: 'Enoch Powell, mate, you are the greatest. You are the don of dons. Get back into Parliament mate and show these cock suckers what it's all about—about all these flash, arrogant, big-mouthed, shouting-their-mouths-off, flash, dirty rapists, grass cunts.

LK: Yeah, fucking rapists and everything.

David Norris discusses suicide with Neil Acourt:

DN: If I was going to kill myself do you know what I'd do? I'd go and kill every black cunt, every Paki, every copper. Every mug that I know, I'm telling ya. I'm not talking about the people I love and care for, I'm talking about the people I don't like. I'm telling ya, I'm telling ya, then I'd just go home and go boom, straight in me head . . . I ain't talking a thirty-foot jump. I'm talking Canary Wharf like, to make sure you're fucking dead.

DN: I'd go down Catford and places like that, I'm telling you now, with two sub-machine guns and I'm telling ya, I'd take one of them, skin the black cunt alive mate, torture him, set him alight . . . I'd blow their two legs and arms off and say 'Go on, you can swim home now.'

NA: Just let them squirm.

Neil Acourt watches a Royal Command Performance:

NA [addressing television]: Black cunt. Get off our fucking royal performances, you.

Neil Acourt and Luke Knight watch Sports Personality of the Year:

NA [addressing television]: Bollocks you nigger. [To Knight]

A macaroon better not win it mate.

LK: I guarantee it's a macaroon. Either Colin Jackson or [Linford] Christie.

Gary Dobson, Neil Acourt and Luke Knight discuss marriage:

GD: You know my mate's daughter married a Paki for a grand, to stay in the country.

NA: For a grand?

GD: For a grand.

NA: She deserves to be kicked up the cunt, mate, and chucked out of a fifth floor window . . . That just shows what a fucking scumbag cunt she must be. What's her mum and dad say?

GD: They can't say nothing about it.

NA: They can. 'Dirty Paki,' mate. 'Get out of our country you Paki cunt.' . . . Fucking hell, if that was my daughter, mate, I'd kill the Paki.

GD: The geezer's a cop. I don't like him.

Gary Dobson describes an incident with a black colleague at work:

GD: There's a nigger there like [i.e. that] me brother used to know years ago. He ain't a nigger but he's black.

NA: He's a black cunt.

GD: He's a black cunt but he ain't, like. Yeah, he ain't a rude boy. He like talks like a normal white geezer, does normal white things, not mug old grannies and things like that, but like he's just one of them type of people who, not on purpose, but like drive you mad, get on your nerves. The other day I nicked his hat. He was getting on me nerves the other day like, he's forever got his hat on. He's like one of the niggers who don't never takes his hat off, so I nicked his baseball cap and he didn't catch me, I got away. He seen me later on and like he got me arm and twisted it behind me back and started mucking about, tapping me on the back of me legs. It weren't hurting but I didn't like it. I just didn't like him doing that and I had the Stanley knife in me pocket, pulled it out and I bit the thing off and I said, 'That'll do there Mick before I end up fucking cutting ya . . . ' All fucking day he was getting on me nerves Luke . . . I said, 'You tap me once more, you silly cunt, I'm going to just fucking slice this down you.' And he let go me arm and said, 'Ah seriously Gary, where's me baseball cap?' He's put like the broomhandle down, 'cos he's picked a broomhandle up. He's gone, 'Seriously Gary, where's me baseball cap?' I went, 'All right, since you've asked nicely I give it to ya.' So I go downstairs and say, like, 'Here it is.' He went, 'Ah cheers.'

Neil Acourt and David Norris talk about the murder:

NA: They're presuming we're guilty, saying and saying . . .

DN: For some reason they keep driving us all mad . . . There's a gap in their promotion, that's what, mate.

NA: And they ain't got nothing still . . . The thing that's making me laugh. We ain't done nothing, that's what I mean. There's none of us done fuck all.

Almost as vicious as the dialogue are the images on the videotape. Neil Acourt repeatedly prances around the room waving knives. As he talks or listens, he casually swings a knife over his shoulder in a bowling motion, finishing with a downward stab. Or he slashes the air, or he pretends to stab a friend, stopping just short of his body in a sort of dare. Once he stabs the kitchen door, muttering to himself: 'I am hard. I can punch doors.' Once he leaves the house tucking a knife in his belt. He even gives Luke Knight instructions on stabbing: 'You know this thing, look, you want to just push it in. It goes right in. If you want to just cut somebody you just put that bit on their face and go . . . [slashing motion].' Gary Dobson is also seen playing with a knife, and the whole group are fascinated by, and play constantly with, a stun gun that they have acquired from somewhere.

Mean people, then: menacing, racist, cruel, seeming to live even in their sitting room on the brink of violence. But nowhere do they implicate themselves in the killing of Stephen Lawrence. Could the tapes be used as evidence? Or used usefully? The lawyers for the Lawrences felt that they clearly demonstrated motive. The tapes showed four young men who boasted to each other of their desire to shoot, stab, maim, torture and burn black people. The prosecution believed that they were a powerful addition to its case.

9

But then there was Duwayne Brooks. Of all the extraordinary aspects to the legal aftermath of Stephen Lawrence's murder, none is more remarkable and more obscure than the prosecution of Brooks for the public order offence said to have been committed at the Welling Road anti-BNP demonstration of 8 May 1993. He went on trial in the same month—December 1994—as the Acourt group were videotaped. The case had taken eighteen months to reach court. Here is the sequence of events.

May 1993: Brooks attends the march, which becomes violent. The police treat the disturbances very seriously, make several arrests, and then set in progress a longer-term investigation to identify and prosecute other participants in the violence. Television companies are forced to hand over news film of the violence to help with identifications. Brooks, who is known to the police because of his role in the Lawrence case, is recognized at the demonstration but the police take no action against him.

September 1993: Brooks is identified again from television footage which allegedly showed him taking part in the overturning and burning of a car. He is questioned and charged.

September 1993–December 1994: His solicitor prepares a defence based on the argument that, at the time of the riot, Brooks was suffering from post-traumatic stress disorder caused by the Lawrence murder. The defence would plead in court that he had witnessed and experienced events so terrible, only a fortnight before the offence, that he was not responsible for his actions and that it would be unjust and inhumane to convict him. But the defence is hampered in preparing this case by the long interval between the offence and the charge. Any psychiatric tests done on Brooks in the autumn would shed only limited light on his mental state on an afternoon in May. So the defence prepares a further argument: that the prosecution is 'an abuse of process', because the delay in pressing charges had seriously impaired the ability of the defendant to defend himself, rendering a fair trial impossible.

When the case reached court, the judge, Charles Tilling, immediately warned the prosecution that he did not like the look of their case and that, in his view, there was little chance of a conviction. Did they wish to proceed? The prosecution hesitated, but went ahead. At the end of a trial lasting several days, the judge threw out the case as an abuse of process. Such an outcome is rare, so rare that an irritated Judge Tilling went so far as to say that he had never before in his career had to take such action.

What was going on? The case was brought by the same Crown Prosecution Service that had rejected the case against the Acourt gang. The CPS, as the Lawrences knew to their cost, can only prosecute if they believe a prosecution to be in the public interest and likely, on balance, to succeed. The public interest argument in the case of Brooks was, presumably, that he had taken a prominent part in a demonstration in which people were injured, and that the interests of law and order would be served by punishing him. But this argument was entirely blind to the larger public interest, given Brooks's part in the Lawrence case. If Brooks had been convicted, his standing as the chief prosecution witness would be compromised; he would instantly be presented by the defence as an unstable and violent criminal. If Brooks had been convicted, how would a sentence, possibly in jail, have affected his temperament as a witness? The truth is that the prosecution of Brooks inevitably threatened to compromise any future prosecution of the Acourt group. And anyway it was, as Judge Tilling observed, a very shaky case. Should it have been allowed to go ahead? Few people would argue that the public interest would be better served by jailing a first-time vandal (Brooks had no previous police record) than by convicting the killers of Stephen Lawrence. And the idea that calculations of this kind are not made in criminal prosecutions is a naive one. They are made all the time, routinely; but not, it seems, in the case of Duwayne Brooks.

Although the case was thrown out, it left its mark by generating a set of documents which were to prove very useful to the defence in the Lawrence case. In the spring of 1994, the CPS had circulated a form among police officers familiar with Brooks, inviting them to describe any behaviour by Brooks which was out of the ordinary. Several officers filled them in with descriptions of encounters in the immediate aftermath of the Lawrence killing, mostly testifying to Brooks's anger, distress and hostility to the police. These documents remained on file, to be disclosed to the defence in the Lawrence case when it asked for evidence of Brooks's mental state. Why these documents were assembled in the first place has never been satisfactorily explained (they were not explicitly requested by Brooks's defence), but they would never have existed at all if the process of law had not been abused through the prosecution of Duwayne Brooks.

Now there were two pieces of documentary evidence which cast doubt on Brooks's reliability as a witness: the forms listing his 'abnormal' behaviour and the police sergeant's report of his alleged conversation with him after the identification parade. The Lawrence family and their supporters did not fail to notice that both of them came from official sources.

10

Still, the private prosecution went ahead. It reached its first stage on 23 August 1995 at Belmarsh Magistrates' Court in Woolwich, where, at a committal hearing, a magistrate would decide whether the case should go for full trial before a jury. Reporting restrictions were not lifted. The proceedings were effectively held in camera so that members of a future jury would not be prejudiced by reading about the case in the press. Four young men were in the dock: Neil Acourt, now aged twenty; Jamie Acourt, nineteen; David Norris, who turned nineteen the previous day; and Luke Knight, eighteen. Gary Dobson, twenty, had not yet been arrested or charged because forensic reports relating to him were still pending.

The hearing lasted for more than two weeks. The core of the prosecution case comprised three elements: the testimony of Brooks, the testimony of Witness B, and the videotapes. Brooks testified for more than two days and was thought by his lawyers to have done reasonably well, despite the defence's deployment of all the evidence which suggested his abnormality and unreliability. Witness B did not do so well. The defence challenged his right to testify anonymously, and when the magistrate, David Cooper, rejected the challenge, took the argument to the High Court, only to be rebuffed again. But when Witness B finally took the stand, his credibility was badly dented; he claimed to know Norris well but had failed to pick him out in an identity parade. The defending barristers strongly contested the value of the tapes as evidence: 'The jury who see these tapes in their jury room will say that the persons depicted, in particular Neil Acourt, is [sic] so unpalatable and has such wicked views that he must be guilty because he is the sort of person who would have done it. They will therefore be swamped by the sea of prejudice.' Charles Conway, defending Neil Acourt, admitted that 'I would not be happy if he [Acourt] married my daughter', but insisted that extreme racist views did not constitute a motive for murder.

Michael Mansfield, for the Lawrences, argued that the tapes revealed the existence of a group of extreme racists obsessed with knives—'very close to an urban terrorist group'—and that gestures that they made could be read as heavy hints that, despite spoken denials, they had committed the murder.

The tapes were ruled admissible, but the cases against Jamie Acourt and David Norris were dropped and they were allowed to go free. These two had never been picked out in an identification parade, and the weakness of Witness B together with a contradiction in Brooks's evidence meant that there was no case for either to answer. (Jamie Acourt had walked free from another courtroom a few weeks earlier when he was acquitted of the Greenwich nightclub stabbing charge after pleading self-defence.)

On 11 September, Luke Knight and Neil Acourt were sent for trial at the Old Bailey for the murder of Stephen Lawrence. They were followed by Gary Dobson in December. Forensic tests had matched a fibre found on his jacket to one from a bag Lawrence was carrying when he was stabbed.

Outside the courtroom in Woolwich, Doreen Lawrence read a statement. 'No family should ever have to experience the last two years of our lives. This is the worst kind of fame. We have been brought into the public spotlight not because of our acts but by the failure of others who were under a public duty to act. The decision of the court today stands as the first clear indictment of that failure.'

The trial at the Old Bailey, London's Central Criminal Court, opened (and closed) in April 1996, and provoked considerable media attention: this was the climax of a three-year struggle by grieving parents, against overwhelming odds, to see justice done. The prosecution case, in brief, amounted to this:

Neil Acourt had been identified by Brooks as one of the attackers. Witness B, who knew the Acourts, also recognized one of the brothers, probably Neil, running from the scene. The video recordings showed that he was a violent and sadistic racist who was obsessed with knives and regularly carried one on the street. The search of his home had turned up an armoury of weapons.

Luke Knight had also been identified by Brooks. He was a known associate of the other defendants and the video recordings showed he was a fervent racist. He had lied to police during interviews.

Gary Dobson had told contradictory stories about the knife found at the home of his girlfriend, Gaynor Cullen, and this knife was one of two in the case which were consistent in size and shape with the weapon that killed Lawrence. A jacket found at Dobson's resembled one described by Brooks as worn by one of the attackers, and fibres found on this jacket were identical to fibres from a bag carried by Lawrence. The video showed that Dobson was a fervent racist who played with knives and had threatened a workmate with one. He was a close friend of the other defendants and had lied to police during questioning.

There was a further, unknown element. Knight and Dobson had both given alibis to the police (Neil Acourt had always said nothing) and it was just possible that they might testify in their own defence. This would give Mansfield the opportunity to cross-examine them. It was not the strongest prosecution case ever to come to court, but the defence case was in some respects weaker, since the three men in the dock had never offered any convincing account of their movements on the night of the murder. The judge in this case was Mr Justice Curtis, and the jury was composed of twelve white people, seven men and five women.

Mansfield began by calling minor witnesses, including the French au pair who was at the bus stop. These witnesses corroborated various parts of Brooks's story. Then Brooks himself took the stand and recounted the events of Well Hall Road.

And that is where, for practical purposes, the Stephen Lawrence murder trial ended.

On the second day of Brooks's testimony, as the defence opened its challenge to him, the judge sent the jury from the room and legal arguments began. These ran for a further day, after which the judge gave a ruling. The evidence of Duwayne Brooks, he declared, could not go before the jury. He then gave his reasons.

Brooks had been diagnosed as suffering from post-traumatic stress disorder but had refused treatment; he admitted thoughts of revenge for Stephen's killing; he made a confession to a police officer which tainted his evidence from the identification parades. 'I am entirely satisfied,' the judge said, 'that where recognition or identification is concerned he simply does not know . . . whether he is on his head or his heels. Nearly three years on, in effect, he has identified three, if not four [different] people as the stabber.' He went on: 'However horrific the crime, however objectionable the motives for it may be, that doesn't in any way enable a judge to remove or alter the legal safeguards held in place to prevent—so far as is humanly possible—the conviction of anybody on misidentification.' To put such evidence before a jury 'would be an injustice, and adding one injustice on top of another does not cure the first injustice done to the Lawrence family'.

When Doreen Lawrence heard these words she collapsed, and later left the Old Bailey in a wheelchair. It was Wednesday 24 April, three years almost to the day since the murder. The family and their lawyers reviewed their position overnight and the next morning dropped the case. The judge ordered the jury to return not-guilty verdicts and Acourt, Knight and Dobson walked free, smiling as they left the court. The jury never saw the videotapes. The three accused never testified.

11

It looked like the end: what more could the Lawrences do? But there remained the unfinished business of the inquest. Adjourned in December 1993, it could now, with the private prosecution concluded, resume its hearing into the cause of Lawrence's death.

It met again in February 1997, at Southwark Coroner's Court under Sir Montague ('Monty') Levine. Coroners are not noticeably celebrated people; they lack the wigs and robes, the whimsical manner and the sombre power ('the full majesty of the law') which have enabled so many English judges to join the club of English eccentricity. Sir Montague, however, had always done his best to add a little colour to the bench, and if coroners can be famous, he was certainly the most famous. He had a large, swirling moustache and wore a flower in his lapel. 'Raffish' was a word that stuck to him. He tended to take a liberal view of his responsibilities as a coroner and he was soon to retire. The Lawrence inquest was one of his last. All five of the originally accused—the Acourt brothers, Dobson, Knight, Norris—had been summonsed to attend.

Doreen Lawrence was among the first to take the stand. This was her first opportunity to speak in a court about Stephen's death and she used it to attack injustice in Britain. 'When my son was murdered,' she said, 'the police saw him as a criminal belonging to a gang. My son was stereotyped—he was black, then he must be a criminal—and they set about to investigate him and us. My son's crime was that he was walking down the road looking out for a bus that would take him home. Our crime is living in a country where the justice system supports racist murderers against innocent people.' The Old Bailey trial, she said, had been a travesty whose outcome had been decided before a word was spoken, and the effect was to make clear to black people in this country that before the law their lives were worth nothing.

Then the five young men were each called to testify, 'to help the court', in the official phrase, to establish the truth. Like Mrs Lawrence, they too had never spoken in court before about the Lawrence murder. Nor did they do so now. On the advice of their lawyers, all five invoked the privilege in English common law not to say anything which might incriminate them—which, in their case, meant saying nothing at all. Every exchange followed the same null pattern.

Question: Were you present at the scene of the murder?
Answer: I claim privilege.
Question: Are you prepared to assist with the investigation

into the circumstances of the death of Stephen Lawrence?

Answer: I claim privilege.

Question: Do you recognize that the murder of a person for no other reason than the colour of his skin is particularly serious?

Answer: I claim privilege.

Question: You have decided to come here and say nothing?

Answer: I claim privilege.

There was laughter in the courtroom when one of them claimed privilege rather than confirm his name, and again when another refused to say whether he played football. It appeared to many people, and was presented by Michael Mansfield, as a mockery of justice.

Sir Monty instructed the jury of six men and four women that they had no choice but to return a verdict of unlawful killing. After half an hour in the jury room they came back with that verdict, but then went well beyond their remit by declaring that Lawrence had been the victim of 'a completely unprovoked racist attack by five white youths'. It was almost as if they had said: 'Had those five young men been before us on a charge of murder, we would have found them guilty.' But this was an inquest and not a murder trial, and the five walked from Sir Monty's courtroom as free as the people they brushed past on their way out.

The refusal of the five to testify and the verdict of the inquest jury had been remarkable enough; but the next day, 14 February 1997, there was a turn in the Lawrence affair that nobody could have predicted. The *Daily Mail* published a front page with a one-word headline, MURDERERS, above mugshots of Gary Dobson, Neil Acourt, Jamie Acourt, Luke Knight and David Norris. A second, smaller headline under the mugshots read: 'The *Mail* accuses these men of killing. If we are wrong, let them sue us.' By the fourth paragraph of the piece it acknowledged that 'one or more of the five may have a valid defence', but went on to say that if any were innocent 'they now have every opportunity to clear their names in a legal action against the *Daily Mail*. They would have to give evidence and a jury in possession of all the facts would finally be able to decide.'

The *Mail* is Britain's largest-selling tabloid in what's known as the 'middle market', and is generally regarded (at least until this year's general election) as a sure divining rod of the mood of middle England. It has, or had then (its proprietor, Lord Rothermere, later switched his personal support to Tony Blair), assertively right-wing, populist instincts: Mrs Thatcher remained its hero. Many liberals were surprised that it was the *Mail* of all papers that was riding so bravely and recklessly to the cause of the Lawrences. Two explanations surfaced in newspaper gossip: that the *Mail*'s editor, Paul Dacre, knew Neville Lawrence because Lawrence had worked as a plasterer during the renovation of Dacre's home; and that, during the inquest, some senior *Mail* journalists had lunched with the Metropolitan Police Commissioner, Sir Paul Condon, and gathered the impression that at least some among the five were guilty. The first story, though unlikely, is true, and Condon certainly met some journalists from the *Mail*. But the explanation inside the *Mail*'s offices was different and more plausible. Dacre was simply incensed by the behaviour of the five at the inquest—being angry and mobilizing anger is part of the paper's emotional ethos—and seized the chance to carry on where the inquest jury had left off. His paper was not standing up for 'black rights'—four years earlier it was the *Mail* which had castigated the people who believed in such things for 'hijacking' the Lawrence case. It was attacking five people—'scum' was the word in the *Mail*'s office—who by their behaviour at the inquest seemed to be flouting British justice, British fairness, British law and order, in all of which the *Mail* believes deeply.

How much did the *Mail* risk? England's libel laws can be punitive. A successful libel action could have cost the paper several million pounds. On the other hand, pursuing a libel action is famously expensive. Getting a case to court costs about £100,000, on average, and that is before the real expense of barristers' appearance fees begins. And there is no legal aid, no subsidy from the state; the five accused by the *Mail* would have had to fight the case with their own money. In a financial sense, the only realistic route open to them was to sue for 'malicious falsehood', for which legal aid is available, but an action for malicious falsehood requires complainants to prove that they have suffered loss rather than, as in libel, simply damage to their reputation. There was no surprise, therefore, when the five did not

Brian Cathcart

sue. The far greater risk to the *Daily Mail* came from the law of contempt, which could be invoked by the Attorney-General. The five had, at various stages in the legal process, been acquitted. Evidence against them had been found wanting. What was the *Mail* doing if not showing contempt for the law and, potentially, interfering with its future course? But the Attorney-General did not intervene.

'We will never give up on this inquiry,' said Assistant Commissioner Ian Johnston after the Old Bailey verdict. 'We will never close this case and we will go on looking forever.' But whatever the police might find, and whatever the newspapers say, Neil Acourt, Luke Knight and Gary Dobson can never again be charged with the murder of Stephen Lawrence, and it would be surprising if a new prosecution were mounted against Jamie Acourt and David Norris—not least because the *Mail*'s front page would be held to have made a fair trial unlikely; any jury would be prejudiced. Could they be tried or sued on a different charge? After the inquest verdict, the Lawrences and their lawyers began to lay plans for a private civil action against the five for injury—shades of O. J. Simpson but with the colours reversed—at which it was hoped that the five could be made to testify. But in practice the standard of proof required would be the same as in the criminal prosecution.

12

There is another question that comes out of the *Daily Mail*'s front page. How would we feel if, rather than five white faces staring out from under the label of MURDERERS, the faces were black? Assume, say, that a white boy had been murdered in Eltham, that a respectable, working-class white family had struggled for years to get their case before a jury, to be beaten in the end by the laws of evidence. Assume that the family 'knew' and the police (eventually) 'knew' that five black boys had done it. And therefore that the *Daily Mail* also 'knew'—they were 'scum' after all—and pilloried them on the front page? How would we feel then?

I think the answer is that liberal opinion, divided over the sight of five white faces below the headline MURDERERS, would have been united in outrage at the sight of five black faces in a similar context. The law does not and cannot 'know' guilt by osmosis; it needs to establish it by proof. The *Mail* would have been accused of usurping what was the proper function of the law and the law alone. I think that, in this hypothesis, the outrage would be justified. But I also think that it is the wrong question, because the hypothesis doesn't work. You have to do more than imagine Lawrence as a white boy. You have to imagine him as a white boy in a black country, with a black police service, a black Queen, black judges, a black imperial history. You have to imagine him living in a black part of south-east London, where the harassment of whites is routine and hatred of whites can be vicious. And then you have to imagine his family being pressed again and again by black policemen about his character and his habits while the black streets which sheltered his black killers went unexamined by a search for evidence that began too late.

This negative of the print of Lawrence's life is very difficult to imagine—the world would need a different history.

The lesson of the Lawrence case, or at least what an examination of it has taught me, is that the law flatters itself when it talks, as it still does, of all people being equal before it. If you toss a coin many times and it keeps coming up tails, then sooner or later you are bound to take a close look at the coin. The history of the Lawrence case is an equally improbable sequence, a succession of events and decisions each of which in isolation can be reasonably explained, but which taken together simply defy the odds. The Lawrence family and their supporters have looked at the coin, and what they have seen is racial weighting. Who can say that they are wrong?

The Acourt brothers, Gary Dobson, Luke Knight and David Norris are all in their twenties now. They still live in south-east London, in or near Eltham, although most of them have moved from the homes they lived in at the time Stephen Lawrence died. They are still occasionally seen together, but they have never spoken publicly about that night. Duwayne Brooks, too, has moved on. He has no wish to tell his story again, having told it so often and never, when it mattered, been believed. The Lawrences have left the home they owned on the Nightingale Estate, but they have not given up. In June this year they met the new Government's Home Secretary, Jack Straw, and the following month Straw ordered an independent investigation headed by a senior judge with the power to force witnesses to testify. Whoever gives evidence in this inquiry, and whatever they say, nobody is likely to go to jail. □

IVAN KLÍMA
DON'T FORSAKE ME

Bára

Bára went to the church on the advice of her friend Ivana. She had been suffering from occasional bouts of depression. Although she had only just turned forty, she put it down to her age, as well as to her less-than-successful second marriage and the feeling that on the whole her life seemed an aimless slog.

The fact was she had suffered from mood swings and sporadic feelings of desperate hopelessness from early adolescence. When she was seventeen she slashed her right wrist in the bathroom at home. She didn't do this because of an unhappy love affair or for any precisely definable reason. Fortunately, her sister Katka found her while she still had a drop of blood in her veins. When they asked her at the mental hospital why she had done it, she was unable to reply. She could simply see no reason for living when life led nowhere but to death, and there was no way of attaining the things one believed worthwhile. What do you consider of greatest worth, the psychiatrist had asked her? She had wanted to reply 'love', but the word was so hackneyed, so devalued by pop songs of all kinds, that it no longer corresponded to her conception of it. So she said nothing. But she promised the doctors and her mother that she would never do anything like it again, and she kept her word. Another spell in a mental hospital, she maintained, and she would definitely go mad.

She really made the promise only to the doctors and her mother; she promised nothing to her father. She had no love for her father and in the last years of his life she scarcely talked to him. She considered her father ordinary: he wore grey clothes, worked as an insurance clerk, told silly risqué jokes, and read detective stories, when he read anything at all. When she was still small, his relationship with her alternated between two extremes: either bringing her chocolate bars and custard puffs, or using death to scare her. Death would come for Bára if she was naughty, if she didn't clean her teeth, if she climbed on the window sill, if she didn't look both ways before crossing the road, or if she cried because she didn't want to go to nursery.

'What's death?'

MAGNUM

189

'Death is like the darkness,' her father explained. 'When death comes for you, you'll never see the sunrise again, the moon won't shine for you, and not even a single star.'

'And can I really die?'

'We must all die,' her father said, visibly pleased that he had managed to frighten her.

'But you'll die before me,' she had told him, 'because you're old.' To her surprise, the prediction made her father laugh.

Apart from a feeling of aimlessness, Bára also suffered from a sense of her own inadequacy, and the paltriness of her pointless existence. There were no real reasons for her feelings: she was an exceptional woman to look at, her tall build and large breasts were the envy of most of her fellow pupils at school. She had her father's fine hair which was of a fairly restrained blonde hue, but which, when the light caught it, acquired a deep coppery tint. She had her mother's eyes: set wide apart and the colour of forest honey. She had acting talent, a beautiful soprano voice, wit and a distaste for anything that could be regarded as humdrum and ordinary, whether in conversation, dress or art. She adored whimsical and outlandish pranks, like the time when she and her friends dressed themselves up in winter clothes on a sweltering summer day and, with woollen bobble caps jammed on their heads, paraded through Prague with skis over their shoulders to the astonishment of passers-by. The very next day they were sunbathing half-naked by the windows of the classroom. She also enjoyed drinking. When she was hard up she made do with beer; as soon as she could afford it she preferred cheap wine.

She had scarcely reached puberty, which happened around her thirteenth year, when she started to draw the attention of all kinds of men, from her own age group up to men old enough to be her father. But nothing convinced her that she was worthy of genuine interest, let alone love and admiration.

She married when she was nineteen. She tried to persuade herself that it was because she was attracted to the man, but more likely it was because she wanted to leave home. Filip, her first husband, was closer to her father's generation, though he was nothing like her father, which was probably what attracted her most to him. He had an interesting and manly job—airline pilot—and spoke several languages; was a good tennis-player and an equally good dancer. Admittedly, he did have one thing in common with her father: he liked to talk about death, not hers but his own—one day his plane might crash. When he first told her this, she clasped him in her arms and begged him to give up flying as she was afraid for him. Her fear evidently excited him because from then on he would take pleasure in recounting to her the disasters that had cost his colleagues their lives.

At the time of their marriage, she was in love with him and genuinely anxious about him, to the extent of going to meet him at the airport during the first few weeks. He loved her too and prided himself on having such a young, beautiful and interesting wife. As he flew on overseas routes, he used to bring her expensive (and to most people in the country, inaccessible) gifts. When, in time, he noticed that her devotion exceeded the level of affection he was accustomed to, he fell prey to the usual masculine vanity. Bára was his property, a mere accessory to his perfection. He started to treat her with increasing unkindness, constantly dwelling on her faults: she wasn't punctual, she lacked purpose and didn't even pass muster as a wife (she paid too much attention to studying instead of to him) or, later, as a mother. Little Sasha screamed (because of her, naturally) often almost the whole night through, when he needed to sleep so as to be fresh for work the next day. He crushed the last remnants of any self-confidence she had. When she discovered that while she was spending her days and nights (or at least that was how it seemed to her) looking after him and his little boy, he was off making love to some air hostess, he explained to her that it was her fault for not creating a proper home.

She rushed straight back to her mother. Was it possible, she asked her, that men could be so mean, so blind to anything but themselves, so selfish, that they were incapable of seeing a true picture of the world or of their nearest and dearest? But her mother was too devoted to her own husband to accept such a generalization. She counselled Bára to be more patient, as she too had been patient.

Bára now began to think about doing away with herself after all, of entering the darkness for good and making a thorough job of it this time. The trouble was, things had changed: now she had a son to consider. So instead of killing herself she got a divorce. Shortly afterwards she fell in love with a man with a biblical name, a builder of Towers of Babel, as she used to call him. At that time, Sasha was three and Samuel forty-three. He was two years older than her first husband, once divorced (he would divorce a second time for her sake) and had a daughter from each of his marriages. She married him—she was convinced—out of love; she admired him and for a long time believed she had found the very best of men. She gave up her acting studies on his account and transferred to a course in architecture. Almost every day during the first months and even years after their marriage, they would talk about the work that united them. Mostly about his projects, which were surprisingly unconventional and liberal for their time. They would also pore over the specialized foreign journals that he was able to get hold of, and discuss—she with greater tolerance, he mostly with his own particular kind of haughtiness—all the various architectural and building projects around the globe.

When she had completed her studies, she realized that while they might share the same opinions about new materials and how the building of high-rise, prefabricated housing estates was a crime, on the most essential thing they would never agree: for her, the most important thing in life was the man she loved, whereas for him it was his work, or rather, success in his work—in other words, his career. Compared to her first husband he was more cultured and well-mannered, but he increasingly required her to subordinate herself to the routine and lifestyle to which he had become accustomed. What this routine required from her was to minister to his comfort. Its aim was to ensure him peace and quiet for his work. They had a son, but for Bára and this boy there remained little time in his life and even less enthusiasm. For his stepson there was nothing at all; he had to make do with a place at the table and a bed to sleep in. At first Bára strove to satisfy his requirements in an effort to wring out of him a recognition that she wrongly confused with love. There was never any acknowledgement; her acquiescence merely fed his sense of superiority. She soon realized that her second husband was also selfish and self-centred and she was merely a very young mother caring for an ageing child. Her relative youth simply meant it was an even greater sacrifice.

And so, after a few years of marriage, Bára started once more to be troubled by the thought that her life was slowly slipping away and she was achieving none of the things she longed for. The dusk was gradually falling, the night was approaching and she got less and less chance to enjoy the sun.

At that time she started to imagine love with another man: a kind, unselfish and wise person who did not worship his own ego and would not regard his wife as a mother to look after him. But these fantasies did little to help her, they were so utterly unattainable that they merely left her dejected and she began to suffer bouts of depression again. She resisted the temptation to be unfaithful not so much out of moral conviction but from fear that her husband would kill her if he found out. He was jealous by nature and he grew more suspicious with age. Apart from that, she had no wish to harm someone with whom she had had many good times, with whom she had once been deeply in love and who had given her much.

At the onset of depression she would generally consult a tarot reader whose predictions contained much to raise her spirits: unexpected good fortune or a man who would steal her heart. She even predicted a new marriage. When the depression was at its worst, Bára would lose all interest in life and be terrified of death. She would want to run away somewhere and start something afresh. What was there for her to start afresh, though? And she had nowhere to run to. Besides, she now had two sons and they needed her and she loved them.

In the course of her life she had acquired a number of women friends. When she was in a good mood and managed to snatch a free evening for herself, she would call on Helena, a fellow student from her second period of study. Helena was the sort of person she could go to a wine bar with to drink and chat about nothing in particular. When she needed advice on child-rearing or consolation during desolate periods of marital vexation she would seek out Ivana, who she had known since the time they were both studying acting at the Academy. Even though Bára abandoned the course after the third year and never returned to the Academy, the friendship remained. Ivana never went into acting but got married and had three children in five years. Her hobby was homeopathy. Whenever Bára's anxiety states were at their height she would rush off to her friend who would prescribe her anacardium or pulsatilla, although the remedies never worked. Either Bára didn't take them for long enough, or she hadn't diluted them enough, or she and Ivana were simply not capable of determining her fundamental problem.

All the same, Bára was sure she could find a very precise name for her fundamental problem: lack of love.

What if she were to try going to church occasionally, it occurred to her friend at their last meeting. She didn't attend any church, did she?

It had been a long time since Bára had attended church.

Why?

Most of all because she had stopped believing in God, or at any rate in the one they preached about in church. When she was a little girl she had very much wanted to believe. Even when she was studying she had still tried; in those days to go to church not only meant admitting one's faith, it was also a sign of opposition to those who forbade belief. And then it struck her that what they preached in churches was too rigid, it hadn't changed for a thousand years. The symbol of a man or God dying in pain on the cross placed an almost perverted emphasis on suffering and death.

On the contrary—her friend explained to her—the cross symbolized the fact that death has been overcome. But for Bára, the cross, like an execution block or the gallows, would always symbolize a cruel and violent ending of life.

Ivana didn't feel well enough versed in theological questions to argue with her. But the minister at the church she attended was an excellent man, both wise and interesting. She always came home from his sermons with a sense of having been cleansed. He was a man of love, she said with unusual fervour. What's more, he had many talents—he sang, played the harmonium, wrote poetry, composed music and made woodcarvings. And he had behaved with courage under the old regime; for several years he was banned from preaching at all in Prague. Perhaps he would be able to explain what she found inexplicable.

Bára did go to the church the following Sunday. She didn't make her presence known to Ivana, however, and left during the final hymn. A week later, she did the same. When her friend asked her what she thought about the sermons, Bára replied that she had found them stimulating, but still felt that she was incapable of believing. What people believed in was simply a dream about God coming down among them in order to conquer death. That was how she saw it anyway. Death ruled the whole universe, after all. Nothing, no sacrifice, could alter that.

How could she shake the minister's hand when she wasn't able to believe in what he preached?

But if she were to speak to the minister privately . . .

But he was in mourning, after all. His mother had died. She could hardly bother him at this time. Besides she was always in a rush; Sam would take it very hard if she were to neglect him on a Sunday morning. He always wanted her around him.

Did she think she wouldn't come next time then? Ivana asked.

Bára said she wasn't sure. She concealed the fact that she had already spoken to the minister, that she had given him a lift. Neither did she tell her how he had captured her imagination, not only by the urgency with which he preached about the need for love, but also by the tenor of his voice and his gestures, which she suspected concealed some deep sadness or suppressed passion.

Letters

Dear Reverend Vedra,

Everyone is asleep here at home, except that you don't know where my home is (where else but Hanspaulka?). I can't get to sleep, I'm down in the dumps. It could be the rotten weather or the fact that Samuel told me that I am ruining his life, even though I do all I can to make him feel contented at home. Samuel is my husband, by the way.

I've decided to write to you because you strike me as wise and kind, and I have the impression that you're someone who is capable of listening sympathetically, not because it is in your job description but because you really are someone fired by the love that you preach about so fervently in your sermons. Of course it's possible just to talk about love and most people are capable of jabbering on about it ad nauseam. But I feel that you mean it, which is why I look forward to hearing you every Sunday. Now I miss your words and your voice. There are so many things I'd like to ask you about. Such as what one must do to live in love and freedom, when one is surrounded on every side by something else entirely: the pursuit of money, self-advancement and an awful lot of violence or at least selfishness, as well as male conceit and vanity, and men's craving to assert their own ego at the expense of their closest companions?

Now I'm astonished at my own effrontery, not only in writing to you but in burdening you with these questions, and taking up your time. As if I couldn't make do with hearing you in church.

But if you could spare me a couple of lines I'd be eternally grateful.

Best wishes,
Yours admiringly,

Bára Musilová

Dear Mrs Musilová,

I do not merit the praise you heap on me. When I speak about love I do no more than pass on the most important aspect of Christ's message.

The aim of what we do is to find real love. This was said most beautifully by St Paul: 'Love never fails. But where there are prophecies, they will cease; where there are tongues, they will be stilled; where there is knowledge, it will pass away. These three remain: faith, hope and love. But the greatest of these is love.'

What is one to do, you ask, in order to live in love and freedom, when there is so little of it around one? Do not expect me to speak as one possessed of understanding or capable of handing out prescriptions for how to live.

A life of love is, I suppose, the desire of anyone whose

heart is in the right place. What was so terrible about the old regime was that hatred and struggle were regarded as so fundamental to life. To many this seemed to make sense because at first glance a life of love seems virtually unattainable. It is enough to turn on the television or read the newspaper headlines: terrorism, robbery, fraud, and all those killed in Bosnia or the Caucasus. And that is leaving aside our everyday life. Could we really hurt each other and quarrel the way we do every day if we lived in love? Could we hate people just because they have a different faith, or look different?

Our desires and expectations are often disappointed, however. Instead of striving once again to find love and put it into practice we invent all sorts of alternative goals. We build careers for ourselves and compete with each other, or conversely, we waste time, failing to fill it with something that reaches out beyond ourselves. We often look for someone to blame for our dissatisfaction, not looking inside ourselves, but outside ourselves. We fetter our hearts with many injunctions, taboos and prejudices. Often they are so choked with these things that when an opportunity arises to fulfil something we've yearned for, we don't even notice it. So we just live, become cold, and replace love with apathy or even rancour.

You write about a world that is full of selfishness, money-grubbing, violence and male arrogance. That's what the world looks like to me sometimes. I've noticed that when people start a conversation with me it is often in order to express some bitterness, not to say something kind. If I offer to carry a woman's shopping bag she becomes alarmed. She thinks that I want to rob her, not lend a hand. But these are only superficial observations. Sometimes we can become outraged with those who are actually suffering.

I have no illusions about how difficult it is to live in today's world. Life has never been easy for those who expect it to fulfil their desires. Therefore every morning I try to reflect on what is really important for my life. If it is to continue to be a life of love then I will have to act and behave accordingly. It is not easy to enter the hearts of others. But wanting to love and to live in love means trying to do precisely that. Whether or not we try is solely a matter of our own determination, and this is where our inalienable freedom lies: our inner freedom to determine our own actions.

I see I've gone on a bit—it's a preacher's failing, and yet I doubt whether I've said anything you didn't know already. I ought to add that real love should reach out somewhere. To Jesus, as I believe. That splendid theologian Karl Barth once wrote that 'human life has no meaning without belief in transcendental truth, justice and love which mankind is incapable of creating alone . . . '

My wish is that you manage to live the way you wish.

With best regards,

Daniel Vedra

Dear Reverend Vedra,

You can't know how pleased I was to receive your letter and how much it helped me. For me, love has always been the most important thing in my life even though I have seldom received much of it from others. No, that's unjust. My mother has always been marvellous and maybe the others would have treated me better if I hadn't messed things up myself.

I married my husband, who is successful and highly respected, out of love. I so earnestly wanted that love to last for ever, and still do, and want to remain true to this wish, true to my husband. And yet I watch with horror as that love fades and is replaced by recriminations, quarrels or cold silence. All that remains is a fixed routine: breakfast, shopping, cooking, housework and visiting people together, or even receptions with feigned smiles and bonhomie. I have two sons. Because of my own irresponsibility I deprived Sasha of a father when he was very small. And I now know I must not deprive my little Alesh of his father.

Sometimes I wake up at night with a feeling of anxiety that I have difficulty in describing to you. It is a sense of wasting my life, my only life, my days, each of which is unrepeatable. Yet I spend them emptily, engaged in some duty or other which I mostly don't recognize as such, in a life without love and without devotion, even though I have long conversations about them at home with my husband.

There are times when I'd just like to take myself off somewhere or cuddle up to my husband and beg him to be with me, be mine, do something, save me. But he is asleep and if I did wake him he'd tick me off for bothering him. I only interest him as a component. A component of the home where he takes refuge, where he needs me to look after and listen to him, as well as tidy and cook for him. But am I addressing my plea to the right person? You are happy because you have prayer and someone who listens to you, or at least so you believe. That's a comfort. That is hope.

There is also hope in what you wrote to me and the advice you gave, although I get the feeling that to live according to your advice one definitely needs enormous strength, patience and perseverance.

You have been so kind to me that I take the liberty to ask whether I might be able to come and talk to you about these things some time—whether I'm allowed to if I'm not a member of your church. I know that time is the most precious commodity that we have and were you to spare me a few minutes I would be eternally grateful.

Yours, Bára M.

Written just before midnight on Wednesday in our fair, royal city which neither the Communists nor my husband have managed to disfigure.

Dear Mrs Bára Musilová,

Thank you for your frank letter. I welcome anyone who feels a need to talk to me about 'such things'. I enclose a card with the times you can catch me in my office—it is situated in the same building as the chapel.

And please don't speak in advance about gratitude before knowing what you'll receive.

Yours sincerely,

Daniel Vedra

Ivan Klíma

Daniel's Diary

I've written nothing for almost a month. Have I lost the courage to be intimate with my diary? Or have I found a different form of intimacy?

I definitely don't have the courage to contemplate the consequences of what has happened. A month ago, B. called and asked if I could spare her a moment. There was a note of urgency in her voice and it struck me she had had some misfortune or other. I told her that I would of course find time for her, and straight away if necessary. She then asked if we might meet in the Small Quarter as she happened to have some business there. She described a bistro halfway along Carmelite Street where we could meet.

I arrived there in under half an hour and when I sat down at one of the small tables I could not rid myself of a sense of something unbecoming. Fortunately the bistro was empty, with just a sickly melody wafting from some unseen loudspeaker.

She arrived a little late. She started to apologize in her usual exaggerated fashion and thank me for coming. I ordered wine for the two of us and asked her if anything had happened.

She said she was suffering from depression, a feeling of anxiety that there was nothing permanent in this life, in her life, in people's lives, in the life of the Earth. Not even in the life of the universe.

I pointed out that there was something permanent in life and the universe too.

'God, you mean,' she said and straight away objected that she didn't want any false consolation, that she'd sooner get drunk on wine than on some illusion. Then she spoke about her marriage. It was possible to put up with anything if one had a little support from one's partner. She maintained that she loved her husband but she had no support from him. On the contrary, she had to support him. 'You're different,' she told me, 'you're strong, you don't foist your burden off on to other people, you help them with theirs.'

Just as on the previous occasion, there were moments when I couldn't concentrate on what she was saying but instead simply registered the melody and tonal colour of her voice, and her appearance. I was also distracted by her fingers that involuntarily drummed the rhythm of the obtrusive muzak.

As we emerged from the bistro it was already getting dark. I wanted to say goodbye, but she detained me, saying that her mother lived a short way from there. Her mother was away at a spa and she had the keys to the flat. She had to go and water the house plants; perhaps I might like to accompany her.

I remained silent and she asked if remaining silent always meant just remaining silent. I continued to remain silent.

Her mother's flat is in an old house in the Small Quarter: just one room with a view on to a narrow little courtyard. Old furniture dating back to the beginning of the century, a brass menorah on the high bookcase. On the couch lay a black cushion with a Star of David embroidered on it in white. The room was full of vegetation with a cheese plant in one corner and a dragon lily in a large flowerpot, while fuchsias and pelargoniums blossomed on the window sills.

She went into the bathroom and filled the watering can. She asked if I was cross with her for bringing me there. I told her I wouldn't have come if I hadn't wanted to. While she was watering the plants she spoke to me continuously about how I was a remarkable person, the most remarkable person she had ever met. She said she could sense the goodness of my heart and also my wisdom, that there were words concealed in me that I didn't dare speak. I told her she was remarkable too and that I sensed in her a passionate longing for understanding, compassion and love. I repeated what I had already written to her: that she sought God, but projected her search on to people.

She said: 'I'm just looking for a good man, a living man. I've been looking for you.' She came over to me and instead of backing away and making my excuses, I took her in my arms.

It's strange how at that moment it struck me I'd first set eyes on her the day my mother died. Whose hand had thrust her into my destiny on that particular day?

Then we made love. I felt such ecstasy that I lost awareness of everything but her closeness and tenderness—and conceivably the long-forgotten tenderness that I used to feel with my first wife at such moments.

It was only when I had torn myself away from her that I was struck by the realization of what had just happened, of what I had done, and I was filled with horror and an overwhelming desire for it all to have been just a dream from which I would awake into my usual innocence.

'Blessed is the man who endures trial, for when he has stood the test he will receive the crown of life which God has promised to those who love him. Let no one say when he is tempted, "I am tempted by God", for God cannot be tempted with evil and he himself tempts no one; but each person is tempted when he is lured and enticed by his own desire. Then desire when it has conceived gives birth to sin; and sin when it is full grown brings forth death.'

'Surely we have every right to,' she said, sensing my mood. 'Surely there can't be anything wrong in love, can there?' As we said goodbye, she asked when we would see each other again.

Instead of saying never, instead of saying we couldn't see each other like that any more, I asked her if she really wanted to see me.

'And don't you want to see me?' she said in astonishment. I couldn't find the strength to say that I didn't.

We met there again on four further occasions while her mother was at the spa. More than once I wanted to tell her that we couldn't continue with what had happened, but the moment I set eyes on her I was incapable of saying anything that might separate me from her for good. Whenever we made love she said: 'Love can't be a sin—you know that, don't you?'

I think to myself, yes, but it depends what kind of love, in what circumstances—but I am looking into those dark Jewish eyes, so full of passion and anxiety and pain, and instead of all the things that burden me at that moment I tell her that I love her.

The most terrible thing of all, it seems to me, is that it's true.

She would say: the most terrible and the most beautiful, because it joins that which cannot be joined, and maybe that's exactly the way life operates.

Daniel and Bára

He was already asleep when the phone rang. 'It's me. You're not cross with me for calling so late?'

'I've no idea of the time. It must be midnight, isn't it?'

'I don't know either. I dashed out without my watch. I need to have a talk with you, but I don't suppose you'd be able to.'

'I'm alone at home. My wife is still in the country.'

'Do you think you could come and meet me somewhere?'

'Are you crying?'

'Maybe. I'm awfully upset.'

'Has something happened? Is it the children?'

'No, the children are asleep. Everyone's at home in the warm, only I'm out here freezing in the phone box at the bus stop. It's like being in a glass coffin. But I'd sooner be in a wooden one. Seeing nothing, knowing nothing and then being pushed into the flames where it would be warm at least.'

'I'll come then.'

Half-past midnight. Outside, an unseasonal July chill and the wind chasing clouds across the sky, their edges pallid in the light of the moon.

He catches sight of her in the distance, standing at the bus stop, long after the last bus has gone. She is huddled up in a short blue-and-yellow mottled coat.

He pulls up and opens the door.

'I've got cold hands again,' Bára says, 'and feet too. I'm cold all over and you've come in spite of that.'

He asks her what has happened.

'I ran away. He threw a ruler at me.'

'Your husband?'

'Who else? We were having a row. Over Sasha. But I don't want us to sit like this in the car.'

'I don't know where we could go.'

'So just drive on!'

'All right. Will you tell me what happened?'

'You don't mind the muck spilling on to you?'

'That's why I've come, isn't it? So you could tell me.'

'Didn't you come because you love me?'

'It's one and the same.'

'I know. So take my hand.'

Her hand is as cold as that time she drove him. How long ago was that?

'He can't stand Sasha,' she says of her husband. 'He's always bossing him about, forbidding him things. Calling him a good-for-nothing idler who does no studying and comes in late. And today he yelled at him that he needn't think he'd be going on to university, that he'd maintained him long enough. And I said I'm the one who maintains him anyway, he's my son, and Sam started yelling at both of us that we're layabouts. I sent Sasha away and told Sam that he mustn't dare do that to me. It flabbergasted him that I should have the gall to stand up to him, because after all he is someone whereas I am no more than a flea that has crept into his clothes, a dustbin in which he chucks all his foul moods. He grabbed the steel ruler and hurled it at me. If I hadn't dodged, he could have killed me. Oh God, it's so vile, forgive me. I ran out of the flat but I had nowhere to go. I would have gone to Mum's, but it was too late and she would have had a fright, so I called you.'

'I'm glad you called me.'

'I'll never forget you came for me, that you didn't leave me in that phone box. And now, instead of getting a night's sleep . . . Where are you taking me? To the airport?'

'No, I'm just driving along.'

'I'd fly somewhere with you. Somewhere far away. Somewhere abroad. Somewhere that's warm. Barcelona, say. They're bound to have warm weather there. But wherever I am with you it's warm, your heart gives out warmth. Don't worry, I don't intend to drag you off somewhere or throw myself on you. I'm going home. No, don't stop. Bear with me for a while yet. Drive me somewhere, just for a short while.'

He turns off the main road and draws up in front of a tower block. 'There's an empty flat up there. It belonged to my mother.'

'Your mum died that same day. I know.'

When he unlocks the door he looks up and down the passage, as if fearful someone might see him. But they are all asleep.

Inside the flat, he is aware of the familiar odour that has still not disappeared even in the five months that his mother has not been here.

He helps Bára out of her coat and they sit down opposite each other. She fixes on him a look of total devotion, or at least that is what it seems like to him and he realizes he is pleased; instead of wasting time sleeping he can spend it with her.

'I don't suppose you'd have a drop of wine here?'

'There's not a thing to eat or drink. Nothing but ketchup.'

'It doesn't matter. Why did you sit so far away from me?'

'I'm sitting quite close.'

'I want you to sit closer.'

He moves his chair so that their knees touch.

'There was a time when he really did maintain us,' she said, 'when Alesh was small. But I was the one who looked after them. He didn't have to lift a finger at home. And what's more, in the evenings I would help him by tracing plans. But since the revolution I do as much work as him, maybe more, because I drudge for him at the office, play the occasional bit part on television, and also do the housework. So tell me, what sort of layabout am I? How can he say he maintains my son?'

'Maybe he just wanted to hit out—strike at you somehow. The pain of a slap passes quickly, the pain of injustice lasts longer.'

'But tell me why, why should he want to cause me pain?'

'Maybe he's jealous of your son.'

'Why should he be jealous of my child?'

'You give him love he would like for himself.'

'And don't you find that horrible?'

'It's human.'

'And would you be jealous of my Sasha too?'

'No. No one has the right to deprive another of his share of love.'

'I know. You definitely wouldn't torture me.'

'Don't think about it any more.'

'You're right. I'm sorry. Here I am with you and I spend the time talking about another man. Tell me, do you still remember your first wife?'

'How do you mean?'

'Can you still bring her to mind?'

'Of course.'

'Often?'

'It depends what you mean by often. Less now than years ago. But most frequently I remember times when we were really happy or, on the other hand, when we hurt each other.'

'You're able to hurt someone too?'

'Of course, when I didn't do something she wanted or didn't protect her enough. When we were going out together, we lived a long distance apart, several hours' journey. There were times when I didn't bother to make the trip because I didn't feel like trudging all that way. And once—it was when she was already expecting Eva—she was summoned to an interrogation. And I let her go there and didn't even wait for her outside the office because there were other things I had to do. Whenever I remember that, I feel regret that I didn't stand by her then.'

'But it only bothers you because she is dead.'

'Yes, I can't make up for it any more.'

'You can make up for it with the living.'

'I've tried to ever since.' Then he says, 'And you remind me of her.'

'Do you think I resemble her?'

'No. It's more a sense of familiarity, a sort of intimacy.'

'It must have been awful for you when she died. Didn't it ever strike you as unjust?'

'It's not the business of death to be just, is it?'

'And how about God?'

'God is just, but his justice is not the same as human justice.'

'Do you think there can be two sorts of justice?'

'It's not a question of a different sort, but of a different dimension.'

'You believe in the fourth dimension?'

'I mean the dimension in which God moves.'

'When my sister died I felt it to be an injustice. Why her, of all people?'

'Your sister died? You didn't tell me.'

'It's ten years ago now. I don't like speaking about it.'

'She was the one who found you when you wanted to kill yourself?'

'I only had one sister. Katka was so kind to me. The kindest of all next to Mum.'

'What was wrong with her?'

'Nothing. She got into a skid when she was driving her car. For five days she was conscious and they just thought she would never walk again. Then she lapsed into unconsciousness. They kept her for six more weeks on a life-support machine. When they switched it off, that was that. When does the soul leave the body? When they turn off the machine, or before?'

'I couldn't tell you.'

'Do you think it's fair that good young people should die?'

'Good and bad people die. We all must die.'

'Yes. Ever since then I've known that I can say cheerio in the morning to someone I love and I may never see them alive again. Or they me. It's sad. It's a sad arrangement, don't you think?'

'And how would you like it to be? How would you have life arranged?'

'I'd like to know I have a few days left. For living. For loving you.'

'You're sure to have.'

'How can you tell?'

'I'll pray for it.'

'You'll pray for me not to die yet?'

He nods.

'I prayed for my sister too, that time. But it didn't help.'

'Don't think of death any more.'

'You're right. Don't be cross with me. Here I am with you and I'm talking about death. It's just the mood I'm in. Tell me, will you lie down with me, or are you in too much of a hurry?' She gets up and finds the door to the bathroom without difficulty.

He hears water running. It is most likely rusty. It has been months since he ran any water here. He has never been able to forget his first wife. Particularly during the first years after her death. Maybe that was the reason he was never able to be completely close to Hana. He was grateful to his second wife and he loved her. But he was incapable of loving her like his first wife.

207

It seemed natural to him, in fact, that one could give oneself fully only to one person in a lifetime. What is it that he feels now? Real love? Or has he yielded to some comforting self-deception?

When Bára returns she is wrapped in a towel, in the same way his first wife used to wrap herself. 'I took it,' she says, referring to the towel. 'It belonged to your mum, but she would have been sure to lend it to me if she knew I was here with you and I loved you.' Then she asks him to turn off the light in the room, but to leave the one in the lobby burning as she is scared of the dark.

They make love on the old ottoman that he still remembers from his childhood. 'My darling,' Bára whispers, 'I love it when you put your arms around me. I love your mouth, your teeth, your eyes. They're a greyish blue like the Prague sky. If I didn't have you, if you hadn't come to meet me, maybe I wouldn't be alive now. I need love to live and without it I'd die. Without you I'd die.'

She groans in ecstasy and begs, 'Save me. You will save me, won't you?'

'From what?'

'From all evil. From cruelty. From the world. From me. From death. You can. You can do it. You can do anything.'

'I don't have that power, sweetheart. But I love you.'

'There you are. You have the power of love.'

The light from the lobby falls on her face that seems pale. But her hair has a coppery sheen and her eyes are dark.

'I've already told you I'm not God.'

'One doesn't need God for love, though. Love is in the human heart. In mine and in yours.'

What time can it be? How did he come to be here? Is it a sin? Is he betraying those he loves? Is he betraying himself? Or would he be betraying himself if he weren't here, if he had renounced this moment when the love he feels overwhelms everything?

She puts her arms around him. 'Tell me you don't mind I dragged you out at night.'

'I'm glad.'

'We've never been together at night before. And never the whole night. And we won't be tonight either. But I'd love to wake up in the morning at your side. At least once.'

'So would I.'

'Would you go somewhere with me and spend a whole day and a night with me?'

He looks at her and into her honey-coloured eyes, and she says, 'Yes, it's me!'

'I'd go with you for a night and a day and a night and a day and . . . '

'No, you know yourself it will never happen. And besides, when you woke in the morning you'd notice I had wrinkles, you'd notice I'm old.'

'But you're not old.'

'I'll be forty-one next month. Do you realize how dreadful that is?'

'No, that's not dreadful.' He sits up. The light from the street enters the room. What is dreadful is to live a lie, to deceive one's next of kin—this is what occurs to him, but all he says is that she is still a little girl compared to him.

Bára stretches out her arms as if wanting to draw him to her, but she too sits up. 'You want to go already? All right, I know, we have to.' She embraces him again. 'Don't forsake me!'

'I won't.'

'But you will. You will in the end. Just now you were thinking what a problem I am for you.'

'No, what was actually going through my mind is that I am deceiving my wife and you're deceiving your husband.' He gets up and goes over to the window. The windmill below the window turns silently.

'I know it bothers you. And already I feel a chill down my spine at the thought of what awaits me at home.' She dresses rapidly. 'Maybe he'll kill me one of these days and you won't even find out! And you'll go on preaching how important it is for us all to love each other!'

Daniel was at home, trying to explain to his daughter that fun wasn't the only purpose of living, when the phone rang in the next room.

'Daniel, I'm sorry to be calling like this but something terrible has happened. Sam has gone and swallowed a whole lot of his pills.'

Something like this had to happen, naturally. What they had

done could not go unpunished. He feared the answer when he asked, 'Is he alive?'

'Yes.' Bára hurriedly explained how she had woken up in the night and heard strange noises. She had found Samuel in his room. The noise had been his choking. On the bedside table he had left two empty tubes of his antidepressant tablets. And a farewell note. The first thing she did was call an ambulance. She had been in the hospital until Sam revived a short while ago.

'What did the note say?'

'What notes like that usually say. That he's old and has nothing to look forward to, that he's just a burden on everyone and me in particular. That he feels I yearn for freedom and so he is giving it to me.'

'I'll come and see you.'

'No, not now. I have to go back to the hospital, he needs me there. I just had to tell you, that's all.'

'I'd like to help you somehow.'

'I don't know what you could do to help. There is one thing, though. Tell me you're not cross with me for always adding to your worries, and tell me you won't forsake me!'

Spring is only just beginning. It is raining and a cold wind is blowing; and there are reports of snow in the mountains.

Daniel and Bára are sitting together in the bedsitter and discussing the news. Until very recently, their favourite topic of conversation was love, but now they each have their own worries and they try to mask them with talk. In a few days' time it will be a year since Daniel's mother died, a year since the day he first set eyes on the woman now sitting opposite him.

They both try not to think about the difficulties they face in the world outside this incubator they have created for their meetings.

Daniel has brought Bára a bunch of roses and an art nouveau glass from which she is now sipping wine.

'Why this goblet?'

'Because you came to see me that time.'

'I came because I was miserable and was brooding on death. I found you attractive,' she says. 'You preached about love and I felt you were searching for it like me.'

He kisses her for those words but finds himself unable to rejoice in her love as he did only a few weeks before. Too much has collapsed around them. To get closer to her he has to struggle through the ruins.

Bára mentions that her friend Helena is getting a divorce.

'Why?'

'Her engineer is a drunkard and she couldn't stand being with him any more. And she has fallen in love.'

'Who with?'

'It's immaterial,' Bára says. 'She simply wishes to be with the one she loves.'

Her announcement contains an implicit reproach. 'Everyone's divorcing,' Bára adds.

'Do you think we should too?'

'Maybe we should, but we won't.'

They quickly finish off the bottle of wine—they have little time. Then they make love. Making love at least distances them for a moment from the world in which they move for the remainder of the day, for the remaining days, and they may quietly speak words of love.

Afterwards Bára bursts into tears.

'What's up, my love?'

But Bára shakes her head. She doesn't want to burden him with her concerns, she knows he has enough worries of his own.

'I don't have any worries when I'm with you.'

'I'm happy too when I'm with you. These are my only moments of happiness.'

'But you're crying.'

'I'm crying because I have so little time with you. Because I don't know what to do now . . . Sweetheart, I'm so disheartened, so miserable and you won't protect me, all you do is lure me to you, and then you turn me out into the cold wind.'

Daniel says nothing. Then he asks if there has been any change at home.

Bára tells him that Sam mostly says nothing. He takes tablets that calm him slightly. But he constantly makes it plain that Bára is his misfortune. She disrupts the order of his life, creates commotion and neglects her duties.

'He's sick,' Daniel says.

'Don't I know it. And he always will be.'

'Shouldn't he be in an institution?'

'I can't do that to him. I've seen the inside of one myself and I know what it means. Death would be better than that.'

'Do you want to leave him?'

'Are you, a pastor, advising me to walk out on a sick man?'

'I'm not giving you any advice. I simply asked what you intend to do.'

'You ask me things instead of being with me and saving me. Tell me, why aren't you with me?'

Daniel remains silent. He knows that either he ought not to be lying at her side or he ought to be with her completely. He has known that since the outset, but accepted this offer of escape from responsibility because it allowed him to put off the decision, to rejoice in his new love without having to draw the conclusions which he feared.

'I know,' Bára says as usual, 'you can't be with me when I'm with Sam. And I can't abandon him because he's mentally ill. And it'll be like that till the end. Tell me, don't you think it's terrible that I'll have to put up with this torture for the rest of my life? Do you think it can be endured?'

Daniel says nothing.

'I always thought I could put up with anything because I'm strong, but these days it sometimes occurs to me that it will drive me round the bend. Tell me, will God take into account the fact that I stayed with a tormenting husband solely to nurse him?'

'No,' he says.

'Why?' she asks in surprise.

'God has other worries. And anyway you haven't stayed with your husband.'

Bára almost leaps up. 'That's rich coming from you! Why don't you tell me like he does that I torment him and am driving him into his grave!'

Daniel says nothing.

'You're like all the rest,' Bára yells at him. 'You teach and preach and prattle about love instead of doing something about it.

For you, a woman is good for only one thing. Go away, go away, go away, I don't want you any more.' And she starts to sob.

Daniel puts his arms around her and holds her head in his hands, kissing her and telling her he loves her.

At that moment it strikes him that he has already overstepped the limit anyway. He has been treading a completely different path to those in his former life. It's simply a matter of acknowledging it and stopping pretending to himself and to his nearest and dearest. Who is the pretence intended for most of all, who does he lie to most of all? He is too attached to this woman, he has steered his course by her for almost a year now and there is no turning back. He says, 'If you like, I'll stay with you.'

'How do you mean?'

'Exactly what I say.'

'You'll abandon your wife and children?'

He says nothing, but doesn't deny it.

'You're crazy,' she says. 'And what will I do with Sam? Am I supposed to kill him, or what? I told you I can't walk out on a sick man.'

'I'm not asking you to.' He realizes now that Bára will never leave her husband. She will stay with Samuel not because he is sick nor because she has a son by him, she'll stay with him because in a strange way she is bound to him: because of her long years of devotion, because of her fear of him and for him, and because of an unquenchable longing to win back his favour and his love. None of that will change.

'My poor dear love,' Bára says. 'I know I'm awful. I don't know what I want. No—I know I'd like to be with you, but I know it's impossible. In the end I'll ruin everyone's lives, including yours. You were better off a year ago. You had no need to add my worries to your own.'

'That year of my life has meant more to me than you can ever imagine,' he says. 'In spite of all the worries.'

'So don't forsake me yet. Bear with me for a while longer.'

She pulls him down into her abyss, into her dark pit, where the only light comes from her dark eyes. She hugs him, they hug each other and he promises her he'll never leave her.

Before they part they make a date for the following Monday,

as usual. Everything is as it was, except that he has the added burden of a promise.

Daniel's Diary

The house is full of workmen. They are knocking down partition walls, pulling up floors, replacing window frames, making conduits for new wiring. In one of the rooms I pulled up the floor myself and cut out a hole for the cables.

'You don't want to be doing that, Reverend,' the foreman told me. 'That's our job and they'll put it on your bill anyway.'

I told him I was doing it for fun, not to save money.

In fact I was doing it to take my mind off things and to tire out my body. It's a relief to think about nothing but carefully following the outline of a hole. And it's easier to get to sleep at night when your body's weary.

Hana is full of vitality and looking forward to her new work. I realize that I love her. I'm capable of leaving her for a while, but I couldn't abandon her. I think about the other woman and realize that I am capable of being without her most of the time, but I couldn't abandon her either.

The awareness of my duplicity is a constant torment to me, but what if it is simply the human lot? Maybe we have confined our nature with more commandments than we are able to fulfil and torment ourselves with feelings of guilt.

Faith

Daniel announced to the elders his intention to relinquish his pastoral duties for several months. The building of the diocesan centre was taking up too much of his time, and he was also hoping to concentrate on preparing for an exhibition of his carvings that was due to open at the end of spring. Neither of these reasons was the real one, but the elders received his request with understanding.

For his farewell sermon he chose his text from Paul's letter to the Philippians:

Therefore, my beloved, as you have always obeyed, so now, not only as in my presence but much more in my absence, work out your own salvation with fear and trembling; for God is at work in you, both to will and to work for his good pleasure. Do all things without grumbling or questioning, that you may be blameless and innocent, children of God without blemish in the midst of a crooked and perverse generation, among whom you shine as lights in the world . . .

Thus he took leave of them as a good and conscientious shepherd, who leaves the flock entrusted to him in the knowledge that it stands aside from the crooked and perverse world, just as he himself does.

Was such an exhortation, such a challenge, a sign of pride or simply of a yearning for a fairer world? Could anyone be denied that yearning?

Those who yearned to become the children of God, he told the congregation, often looked upon those around them as pitiable wretches, who regarded their stomachs as their god, whose thoughts were earthbound, who took pride in things they should be ashamed of. In other words, they regarded the rest as a crooked and perverse generation. And when we also look at the world around us, it appears to be going to ruin, and the whole of life is being increasingly transformed into a dance around the golden calf. But let us not be haughty or proud, let our hearts not be hardened by our severe assessment of our neighbours. It is not our task to condemn them, it is our task to do our best with our lives and realize that each of us will go astray. Our lives cannot be without blemish, but there is hope for us because the Lord Jesus Christ will not forsake us, in Him we have a light that will shine in the darkness and lead us back out of it.

Daniel spoke and as in a mist he could make out familiar faces; he knew everyone gathered here, knew them by name, knew their life stories, their cares, their jobs, the names of their children.

Large flakes of spring snow swirled outside the window. Like that time a year ago. All of a sudden that critical day came back to him—if it is possible to designate a particular day as a turning point. His mother was dying and he was struggling to rekindle his faith, his belief in the immortality of the human spirit. And into this time of confusion stepped a woman who was destined and willing to transform his life utterly.

His thoughts wandered to the past while his lips spoke of the importance of bringing light into the lives of others. Nothing in life is more important than that. To be a light in the life of your neighbour means more than any wealth, more than any power.

He didn't say that for years he had striven for this, had tried to live that way, and perhaps he had indeed lived that way in spite of all his mistakes. Daniel felt a sudden pang of regret that something of importance was coming to an end, something so important that it was as if his very life was ending. He struggled to control his voice, while at the same time he became aware of a real pain gripping his chest.

He had survived the time of oppression but not the time of freedom.

When the sermon ended, silence descended on the chapel. Had he announced that he was leaving his post for good, someone would be rushing up with a bouquet and a speech of thanks, but he had kept his defection secret, so they all simply waited for him to introduce his replacement. He led her to his place and allowed her to say a prayer and the blessing.

He did not go out into the street; the weather was too bad. So he said goodbye to the congregation in the passage. People shook him by the hand and wished him all the best, voicing the hope that the building work would soon be successfully completed and that he would also enjoy success with his carvings. Everyone wanted to know the date of the exhibition and he promised to let them know in good time.

He still had to go to his office to hand over the keys, and he promised that he would, of course, still attend the next few elders' meetings and the Bible study classes. Then he went downstairs to his workshop.

A half-finished carving sat on the small workbench: a man astride a small donkey. Jesus entering Jerusalem. How many artists, both renowned and unknown, had portrayed that event, which may never have happened?

He took the gouges from their case and started to hone them

on a small oilstone before sitting down to carve.

A few days earlier the gallery owner who had promised him the exhibition had visited to ask how the preparations were coming along. He had also taken a look at the latest carvings and seemed to be delighted with them. The figures were not just better from a technical point of view, they were also more expressive, their features conveying a quality of mind and emotion that was almost tumultuous.

The gallery owner's praise had gratified him although he ought to have told him that the mental and emotional turmoil in the wood reflected a far more passionate and tumultuous agitation in his soul.

He had preached today for the last time. He had told no one, not even himself, but he knew now that he would never return to the pulpit. Was it because of the woman who had entered the chapel unexpectedly and uninvited?

No, he had brought it on himself; the woman simply stood at the end of a path he had embarked on a long time before she appeared. He had been guilty of deception before then, when he had concealed his doubts about the fundamentals, about the message he brought and about the Christ whom he proclaimed.

His only excuse was that he had deceived himself too. He wanted so much to believe in everything he preached, to believe that God assumed human form, that He suffered, that He died on the cross, that He descended into a vague and unimaginable hell and on the third day rose again from the dead. That He ascended into a heaven that was situated in a vague and unimaginable space, and there sat down at the right hand of His Father, God Almighty, where He will remain until the day He returns to earth to judge the living and the dead. Daniel used to convince himself that everything was just the way he preached it, precisely because it was unbelievable and inconceivable. He wanted to believe it because if nothing he preached was true, then life would be no more than a meaningless cluster of days between the beginning and the end, between the eternity that preceded it and the eternity that would come after.

Previously he had trodden paths that people had followed for centuries and now all of a sudden he found himself in the middle of an immense plain devoid of paths. He could set off in any direction. Admittedly he could not see the end of the plain but he knew that whichever direction he took, he would eventually confront a bottomless abyss.

He had done what he could to dispel that image of an open space leading to an abyss that engulfed everything and everyone, but he had failed.

He was conscious of a cold panic, dizziness and gripping heart pain.

He ought to get up and leave this tiny room, go and find his children, his wife, go and make love to Bára. He ought to kneel down here before this unfinished carving of Jesus on a donkey and beg for the gift of faith that alone could dispel the anxiety, bridge the abyss and offer the grace that is denied to all other life.

He didn't kneel down.

The pain in his chest grew.

He got up and walked over to the window. There was a sudden break in the clouds and the heavens were revealed. Beyond them an endless universe. Billions and billions of stars. An infinity of time and space. And astonishingly, there was no place in it any longer—no fitting place in it—for a God who had become man and watched over events on this insignificant planet.

Beads of sweat stood out on his forehead and turned cold; Daniel realized he was beginning to fall. Everything started to rush away from him. And tomorrow he had a date with Bára; how would he get there? He groped around him for something to hold on to.   □

Translation by A. G. BRAIN

GRANTA

JOHN McGAHERN
LOVE OF THE WORLD

It is very quiet here. Nothing much ever happens. We have learned to tell the cries of the birds and the animals, the wing-beats of the swans crossing the house, the noises of the different motors that batter about on the roads. Not many people like this quiet. There's a constant craving for word of every sound and sighting and any small happening. Then, when something violent and shocking happens, nobody will speak at all after the first shock wave passes into belief. Eyes usually wild for every scrap of news and any idle word will turn away or search the ground.

When the Harkins returned with their three children to live in the town after Guard Harkin's heart attack on Achill, they were met with goodwill and welcome. The wedding of Kate Ruttledge to Guard Harkin, ten years before, had been the highlight of that summer. A young, vigorous man struck down without warning elicited natural sympathy. Concern circled idly round them—would Kate take up work again, would he find lighter work?—as if they were garden plants hit with blight or an early frost. The young guard, an established county footballer with Mayo when he came to the town, was tipped by many as a possible future all-star. We'd watched Kate grow up across the lake, go away to college in Dublin and come home again to work in Gannon's, the solicitors, turning into a dark beauty before our eyes. She was running Gannon's office at the time they met, and was liked by almost everybody. The excitement that ran through the town and near countryside when Harkin declared for the local club was felt everywhere. Excitement grew to fever over the summer as he led the team from victory to victory, until he lifted high the beribboned silver cup in Carrick on the last Sunday in September. Nineteen long years of disappointment and defeat had been suddenly kicked away, and the whole town went wild for the best part of a week.

Kate, who had shown no interest in sport of any kind up till then, spent every Sunday of that rainy summer travelling to football matches all over the country. She'd seen Harkin prostrate on the field at Castlebar when Mayo lost in the Connacht Final, but everywhere else she attended was victory and triumph. She'd witnessed men and boys look long and deep into his face, lost in the circle and dream of his fame. She'd held her breath as she'd seen him ride the shoulders of running mobs bearing him in triumph from the pitches. There were times when he fell injured on the field, and she could hardly breathe until she saw him walk again when he was lifted to his feet.

On an October Sunday at the end of the football season Kate took him out to the farm above the lake to meet Maggie and James for the first time. They parked the car at the lake gate to walk the curving path through the fields above the water and down to the house in its shelter of trees. Girls didn't take men to their homes at the time unless they had made up their minds to marry. These visits were always tense and delicate because they were at once a statement of intent and a plea for approval. There was little Kate had ever been denied. Now all her desires and dreams were fixed on this one man. In her eyes he stood without blemish. These small fields above the lake were part of her life. Away from here she often walked them in her mind, and, without her noticing, this exercise had gradually replaced the earlier exercise of prayer. She was light, almost tearful with happiness as she closed the lake gate. Now she was leading her beloved through the actual fields to meet the two people who meant most to her in the world, and she felt as close to Harkin and as certain of her choice as she was of her own life. The lake below them was like a mirror. The air was heavy and still. The yellow leaves of the thorns were scattered everywhere with the reds of the briars and the thick browns of the small oaks. Blackbirds and thrushes racketed in the hedges. A robin sang on a thorn.

'What do you think of the place?' she asked as they crossed the hill to go down under the tall hedges to the house.

'It's a bit backward and quiet,' he said. 'The views, though, are great. They'd pay money to have this in the middle of a city.'

In the house the young guard was polite, even deferential, as he enquired about the fields and the lakes and the cattle. Her father, James, was quiet and attentive, asking in his turn about the sheep and cattle they kept on the Mayo farm the guard had grown up on. Maggie was herself as always, quietly there, large and easy, withdrawing only to make the sandwiches and tea. Whiskey was offered, but at that time Harkin did not drink. Already he felt comfortable in the house. It was a house where he felt he wasn't expected to be anything other than himself. There was a generous side to the guard's nature; among footballers he was known as an unselfish player. After they'd eaten, and he'd praised the tea and the sandwiches, he felt moved in some clouded way to give something of himself back for the simple courtesy he had been shown. The generous virtues are at times more ruinous than vices.

'I don't expect to stay a guard for much longer,' he said. 'I've already passed the sergeant's exam, and I expect to go much further.'

'To get to be a sergeant is a big step,' James responded. 'Not many get that far in a whole lifetime.'

'I expect to be a super or an inspector at the very least. The Force is awash with old fools. It needs a big shake-up.'

The young guard went on to ridicule his immediate superiors and to expand his sense of self to very attentive listeners. When he finished the free run of untrammelled self-expression, he was taken aback by how much time had flown.

The old couple walked their daughter and the guard all the way out to the car at the lake gate.

'What do you think?' James asked his wife anxiously as they made their slow way back to the house.

'There's no use worrying,' Maggie said. 'Kate will have her way. To go against him would only make her more determined.'

'Kate isn't going to have an easy life. She needs somebody easier.'

Maggie pressed his shoulder as they walked. 'When we married, and you came in here, everybody was against it. Yet it worked out all right.'

'I can't help wishing she had found somebody easier. That poor young man is full of himself.'

'There's no use wishing,' Maggie said. 'We'll have to make the best fist of it we can.'

'Still, we sent her to school. She has pleasant work, plenty of friends. I wish . . . I wish . . . ' But Maggie did not encourage him to complete the wish.

All the people who lived around the lake were invited to the wedding. His people travelled from Mayo. They were tall and good-looking, forthright in their manner and very proud of Guard Harkin. Famous footballers came from all over the country and formed a guard of honour outside the church. Girls who had been to college with Kate in Dublin travelled from as far as New York and London, to attend the wedding. The church was full. The whole town turned out. The crowds spilt into the church grounds and even on to the road, and the wedding was talked about long after the couple had gone to live in Athlone. Guards were transferred automatically once they married.

We saw little of them in the years that followed. Harkin's football career was at its height. He was much in the newspapers, and there were pictures of Kate by his side at the celebratory dinners and dances. In all the photos she looked glamorous and happy. For a while Kate had temporary work in Athlone, but James told me that Harkin didn't like to see his wife working. They came for short visits in the winter and a few times appeared with Maggie and James at Sunday Mass where they were the centre of all eyes. At the church gate after Mass people would crowd round them to grasp their hands, and the talk of what Kate was wearing and how she looked and what a nice plain man Harkin was in spite of everything would sound around the place for days. They were admired and envied. Once Kate did come for a visit on her own and must have stayed two or three weeks. I was over helping James with cattle, and we came together into the house. She was wearing a blue dress and sitting with her elbows on the table looking out of the back window towards the old apple tree heavy with green cooking apples. She was far more like a young girl dreaming about her life than a settled married woman. Once she noticed me, she rose quickly and smiled and stretched out her hand. We were cousins as well as good neighbours.

I was told that Harkin was studying hard for the new sergeant's exam. The last time he passed but failed the interview. Now he was more determined than ever.

'Kate says he finds it easier to study when he's on his own in the house,' Maggie said while James sat looking down at the floor without adding a single word.

That summer Mayo won the Connacht Championship and beat an Ulster team to reach the All-Ireland Final against Cork. James and Maggie were offered seats in the Hogan Stand, but used one excuse or another to get out of going. I walked round the lake to watch the match with them on television. Their near neighbour, Michael Doherty, had crossed the fields to watch the match as well. There was a long dry spell of weather that September. The Sunday was warm and golden. All the time I was in the house, the front door was left open on the yard. Outside the back window, the old Bramley was heavy again with cookers. Maggie poured us a large whiskey before the match began and filled our glasses at half-time. When it was over, we all had tea and sandwiches. Mayo lost, but Harkin had played his heart out at centrefield. If Mayo had had even one more player like him, they'd have won. Once we thought we saw Kate's face in the rows of heads in the Hogan Stand. When I got up to leave, James took his hat and insisted on walking me all the way out to the lake gate. Michael Doherty stayed behind to chat with Maggie. We were going in different directions anyhow.

'Thanks for the day, for everything. It would have crowned it had they won,' I said as we parted.

'What's it but a game? We had the day. Thanks yourself for coming all the way over.' James waved, and I saw him wait at the gate until I passed out of sight behind the alders along the shore.

That game and year must have been close to the very best of the Harkins' life together. Kate was expecting their first child. In the new sergeant's exam he came first in the whole of Ireland. He was certain he'd be promoted before the next year was out. Maggie went early to Athlone to help Kate around the birth, and James went for the little girl's christening.

'The little girl is a treasure,' Maggie told me when they got back. 'Outside that, though, things could be better.'

'How could that be? Aren't their whole lives in front of them? He's going to be a sergeant before long?' I asked though I wasn't all that surprised by what she said.

'He's not so certain now. When he walked into the room for the interview, whom did he find sitting behind the table but the same officers who turned him down the first time.'

John McGahern

'How could they turn him down after him coming first in the whole country?'

'He says that if they're against you enough they'll turn you down no matter what. There were no older guards at the christening, just foolish young fellas who looked up to him as if he were God. Even if you have to come in first everywhere, you must learn to wait and bide your time along the way. A man can only do so much; after that, it's people who do everything. When God made us, He didn't allow for us all to be first all the time.' The words were very strong coming from James.

I saw Maggie look hard at him as he spoke. When he caught her eye, he stopped; nothing more was said, and I asked nothing more. Harkin came with Kate and the child a few times to the farm that year but did not stay for long. They never appeared together at Mass. Another girl was born the following year. Maggie went to help Kate as before, but this time James refused to go to Athlone for the christening. Harkin was no longer playing football. A nagging knee injury had worsened, and he had no interest in continuing to play at club level. He joined a gun club with a new friend, Guard McCarthy. He also started to drink.

'I couldn't wait to get away,' Maggie said when she came home. 'I fear Kate knows now she has her work cut out.'

In spite of what she said, she went again to Athlone to help Kate with her third baby, a boy. It was a difficult birth, and Maggie was several weeks away. During this time, Michael Doherty crossed the fields nearly every night to sit with James for company. When Maggie was at home, he came to the house a number of nights each week but not as frequently as when she was away. Some weeks after Kate's son was born, he stopped in fear when he came into the yard to find the house in darkness. The door was open. He switched on the lights. The rooms were all empty. There was a low fire in the cooker. Outside he heard a dog barking in the fields and then a tractor running. He found the body lying by the transport box. The ground all around was trampled, but the cattle hadn't walked on the body. James had scattered the hay before falling. Each of the baler twines had been cut.

James had married into the place and he cared for the fields more than if they were his own. Not only were he and Maggie

226

man and wife but they were each other's best friend. 'I should never have been away. I should have been at home minding my own business,' Maggie complained bitterly for months and could not be consoled.

'You shouldn't take it so hard. A boy has come in so that an old man can go out,' one of those foolish people who have a word for everything said.

'He was not old to me,' she cried.

Harkin was in the newspapers again, but not the sports pages. He had been with his friend Guard McCarthy late one night when their patrol car was called to a disturbance at an itinerant encampment on the outskirts of the town. A huge fire of car tyres and burning branches lit up the vans and mobile homes, the cars and mounds of metal scrap. Stones and burning branches were thrown at the Garda car. They radioed for reinforcements before getting out.

The guards said that as soon as they left the car they were set upon by youths and men wielding sticks and iron bars. All the itinerant witnesses swore that both guards had jumped from the car with drawn batons and provoked the assault. In the bloody fight that followed, the guards stood and fought back to back, the short, leaded batons thonged to their wrists. When the reinforcements arrived, three tinkers lay unconscious on the ground. The rest of the men had escaped into the fields, and McCarthy and Harkin were being attacked by a crowd of hysterical women. McCarthy's face was covered with blood. He had a serious head wound. An ear hung loose. Harkin's left arm was broken, and he was cut and bruised.

When one of the tinkers died in hospital without recovering consciousness, a terrible furore started in the newspapers, on the radio and television. Itinerants' rights organizations denounced the two guards and Garda treatment of itinerants in general. At the trial the guards were exonerated of criminal wrongdoing. Whether excessive force was used or not remained unanswered. Once the uproar subsided, an internal Garda inquiry was held after a civil action brought by the itinerant families was settled out of court. As a result, McCarthy was transferred to a coastal town under the

Cork–Kerry mountains. Harkin was sent to Achill Island. Any lingering hope he held of advancement in the force was gone.

On Achill the heart attack came without warning. For several weeks it was touch and go whether he'd live or die. He came through a number of serious operations. Strangely, he was very happy in hospital and an ideal patient. By the time he was released it was known he'd never be fit to resume normal police duties. For the first time in a marriage that had slowly emptied of everything but caution and carefulness and appearances, Kate took a decisive part. If Harkin accepted the desk work he was offered in a station in one of the big towns, he would have to go there alone. With him or without him Kate was going back to what she knew.

It was one of those rare moves in life which appear to benefit everybody. Maggie made no bones then or later that Kate saw it as a last chance to climb back into some kind of life of her own. The town had not won a county championship since that great summer ten years before, and Harkin was greeted like a returning idol.

He had been deeply shaken by the way people turned away from him once he ceased to be a star, the same people who had crowded around him on pitches and in hotel lobbies, had stopped him in the street to ask for autographs. This constant attention had been so long a part of his everyday life that he had come to take it as much for granted as air or health. When suddenly it disappeared, he was baffled: he was the same person now as when he had dominated centrefields, and it gnawed at the whole structure of his self-esteem, forcing in on him the feeling that he no longer amounted to anything, he who had meant the world to cheering, milling crowds. Back in this small town where he was well remembered he felt he could breathe again, and the welcome and sympathy he was shown soon brought immediate, practical benefit.

During the ten years the Harkins had been away, tourism had grown rapidly. There were now many guest houses, and foreigners had built summer houses by the lakes and were buying and converting old disused dwellings. They were mostly Germans and French, with a scattering of Swiss and Dutch: highly paid factory workers from industrial cities, attracted more to the hunting and fishing and cheap property prices than to the deserted beauty of the countryside. A local guard, Guard Tracy, had developed a lucrative sideline looking after their summer houses and soon had more work than he could handle. Some of this he passed on to the disabled ex-guard, with promises to put more business his way if things went well, but when Tracy was transferred suddenly to Waterford, Harkin got control of the entire business. Suspicion grew that he had brought about Tracy's transfer by reporting his dealings with the foreigners to the Garda authorities, but it could as easily have been any one of several people. While Tracy had managed the properties only, Harkin threw himself into the whole lives of the tourists. Soon he was meeting them at Dublin airport and taking them back. He organized shooting expeditions. He took them on fishing trips all over. These tourists did not return their catch to the water. The sport was in the kill. As well as pheasant, duck, woodcock, pigeon, snipe, they shot songbirds, thrushes, blackbirds, even larks.

His damaged heart meant Harkin wasn't able to go with them over the fields. Often he stood on the roads with his new repeater and guarded access to where they were shooting. In the summer they came with freezer vans, and Harkin took them to lakes rich in pike and perch and eel. He helped them net the lakes in broad daylight as well as at night. Heads of gutted pike were scattered round every small shore. Because of his contacts in the guards he was able to obstruct complaints, and most people did not bother to complain. Harkin was well known and admired—the disabled guard was entitled to a living like every other. The lakes had been there for so long and were so little used, except by eel fishermen from the north, that they were taken for granted; but everybody disliked the slaughter of the songbirds. When the day's shooting and fishing was done, the tourists loved to party and drink. In the same way as he disregarded the plunder of the lakes and the growing hostility to the shooting of songbirds, Harkin drank pint for pint, glass for glass, with his new friends without seeming to care for his health. At parties he would pull off his shirt to display the scars of his operations.

At weekends and in the winter evenings, Kate's two daughters often accompanied their father on his rounds of the empty tourist houses, while the boy went with his mother to visit Maggie, sometimes to stay the night. Kate must have felt the changes ten years can bring as she walked the curving path through the fields above the lake and down by the tall trees to the house. It was her son's hand she now held instead of Harkin's, his grip more demanding than ever her husband's had been. All that drowsy love had gone: she feared him now and feared closeness, not distance. The path and the lake and the fields were the same. Her father was gone, his dear presence nowhere but in her mind, and everything continued on as before. The blackbirds and thrushes racketed. A robin sang. Maggie was still there, praise be to everything that moves or sings. A red shorthorn left the small herd and walked with them on the path, frisking its long tail excitedly while trying to nuzzle her hand. 'Will it bite us?' the child asked. 'No. It's just looking for nuts. Your grandfather was always trying to stop your grandmother turning them into pets.'

'You left the two lassies behind today?' Maggie met them, her broad face creased with smiles.

'They went with their father on his rounds of the houses.'

'My little man is in his lone glory, then.' She stretched out and lifted the boy high above her head.

For days at a time and whole nights of the summer, Kate and the children didn't see Harkin, but when they did, he was usually in good humour. He had plenty of money. He had always been generous, and Kate now had more money than she needed. His life became so intertwined with the tourists that in the off-season they sent him air tickets to join them in various cities. Kate thought little of the trips. When he was leaving, she wished him a good holiday and had the children wish him the same. He always brought back presents.

The tourists congratulated him on having an obedient, old-fashioned wife. They raised their glasses and wondered if he could find such a wife for Pierre or Helmut. Harkin took out his notebook and, with the mock solemnity of a policeman raiding a public house for after-hours drinking, wrote down the names, warning each man that anything said could be used in evidence against them once he found them such a wife.

They roared with laughter. 'Harkin can do anything. Harkin is the devil . . . '

As Kate was walking back through the town one morning after taking the children to school, Jerome Callaghan's car pulled up along the curb. He pushed open the door on the passenger side for her to get in. She hesitated. They'd once been in the same class at school. He now owned his uncle's auctioneering business and had a reputation for going with older women.

'I've been looking out for you, Kate,' he said. 'How would you like to work again?'

She was taken aback because it was as if her most secret thought had been taken from her and offered casually back. 'There aren't many jobs for women my age.'

'There's one,' he said. 'They are looking for someone to run the office in the market.'

It was what she had hoped for but had never expected to find in this small place. As they talked, she knew she could do the work. All she doubted were his motives. She refused his offer to drive her home, saying she had things to get for the house. She also said she'd make her own way to the mart for an interview with McNulty, the manager, later the same day.

At twelve o'clock she went to the big galvanized building outside the town in the middle of a huge, gravelled space for cattle trucks and trailers. In spite of dressing with great care, she felt nervous and vulnerable offering herself for work again after all these years. McNulty could not have been more friendly. He seemed to know a great deal already about her training, and after a short conversation offered her the job there and then. He wanted her to begin work the following morning.

Confronted suddenly with an offer she had long wanted but only dared to think about in secret, her first instinct was to back away: she didn't know how her husband would react when he got back; she'd like time to think it over. McNulty couldn't give her time. If she wouldn't take the job, he'd be forced to look for someone else. More than a million pounds passed through the mart each week. She was always free to hand in her notice if, after a few weeks, she found the work didn't suit her.

She began the following morning. Men were already hosing the cattle pens when she came in, the arc light high in the steel girders shining down on the wet concrete. Annie and Lizzie who worked in the office were friendly and helpful. They'd worked in the mart for years and feared that the new person would be hostile or distant; either of them could have done her work, but they didn't want the responsibility. A few of the small farmers, who came in about cheques or cattle cards, she'd known since she was a girl, men like her father, rough and ready and anxious; but her father was not rough, and she knew that much of the rough manner was a shield, a working uniform. The dealers were more polished and better dressed and more interesting, and they too wore uniforms. Cattle she had grown up with. She loved their faces. She found their lowing hard at first, lowing for what fields and company they'd been taken from. They'd be driven round the sale rings, loaded on to trucks or trailers and carried through the night to ships or abattoirs. Only a few would reach the lives of new farms. All that passed through her office were their cards, their bills of sale, the cheques, the dockets. She was so busy on mart days that the voices of the auctioneers calling out their rhythmic numbers over the loudspeakers were only a distant sound.

On mart days and the days that followed, which were even busier, when the accounts had to tally and any irregularities of sale or purchase reported to McNulty, Maggie would come into the town to pick up the children from school. On all other days Kate had time to see to the children herself. As long as the work was done, they didn't care what hours she kept.

The days flew. In the quiet morning after leaving the children at school, as she came up the back lane to the mart by gardens and the yards of the bars and engineering works savouring the morning, she began to realize how much she had missed the independence of work. Now it was through this new concentration—and the simple walk from the school to the mart a prelude to the work itself—that each day had been given back to her in its long light and depth, all the actions and interactions of the day, between the setting out and the returning, a reflection of the mystery of the whole blessed gift of life. She had nearly lost that gift. She had given up thinking of her marriage. Though she had searched for hours, she had never been able to isolate any single day, or even month or incident, when it had taken that wrong turning; but it had turned, and they had never talked. How or when or why would never be known. She had no other wish but to live her life and to bring up her children in peace—without her husband, or any man. With her husband in the house, she felt more alone than in his absence. Her nervousness in the face of his return quickened the speed with which the days flew. They seemed to race. Jerome Callaghan was in the mart most days. When they met, he was polite and careful. Once he asked her how she liked the work.

'I'm very happy.'

'Everybody's delighted with you, anyhow,' he said.

'You can say that again.' Annie looked up from her chair far down the counter and echoed his words so vigorously that Kate knew that they were happy with her work and wanted her to stay. Her husband's visit abroad was prolonged much more than usual. She was relieved at the first postponements, but then her nervousness grew greater in the face of his return. The days no longer raced. They were fixed on his return like a held breath.

Harkin brought many presents back at the end of seven weeks. The three children were very excited, and he was full of plans for making a video of the area with a German company. If the video took off it could bring the many abandoned houses in the mountains on to the market as well as increase interest in the lakes, and it would make sense for him to set up as an auctioneer as well as to expand his present business. They could all wind up as millionaires. He had been drinking earlier in the day but he was far from drunk. Kate knew he would dislike that she had found work and that it was better that he heard it directly from her, but such was the atmosphere of the house and her own deep horror of confrontation that she kept putting it off. As the children were getting ready for bed, having eked out the day well past their usual bedtime, the boy blurted out proudly, 'Mammy's got work. Some days she takes us into her office after school.'

'What sort of work?'

'In the mart—in the office,' she answered quickly.

'Who gave you this work?'

'They were looking for someone in a hurry. Mr McNulty gave me the work.'

'So Horsey McNulty is a mister now all of a sudden. Did you need the money?'

'No. We've never had so much money.'
'Were you short of money before?'
'We were never short.'
'Why did you want the work?'
'The children are growing up. It was a chance to get out of the house.'
'Of course I didn't need to be consulted.'
'I tried to put off taking the job till you came home, but they couldn't give me the time. They needed somebody that week.'

The mood of the house changed. Instead of trying to postpone their bedtime, the three children were anxious to be away and under the blankets. When the doors of their rooms were closed, he took a whiskey bottle from the press and poured a large glass. She was always apprehensive when she saw him drink whiskey.

'Those crowd of wide boys knew well what they were doing. As well as McNulty, Jerome Callaghan is stuck to his elbows in the mart and he's nosing after the one thing.' He suddenly drained the glass but didn't reach for the bottle again. 'You'll have to throw it up. That's all. I'm not going to have my wife working up in the cow shit with a pack of wide boys. It's not as if I don't make enough money. You'll give it up tomorrow and get the hell out of the place.'

She said she couldn't. She liked the work, and it didn't interfere with the running of the house or the children. She said that the people were pleasant, especially the two women who worked with her in the office, and she had given them her word.

With the empty glass in his hand he rose and came towards her. It was as if all the resentments he'd held half in check over years had gathered into a fist. He had married her when he could have had his pick of women. He had given her a house, car, children, clothes—everything a woman could want. What had she given back? Nothing, nothing. She had given him no help at all. Their life had been a dog's life. He hadn't even the life of a dog. 'Have you ever asked yourself if there's anything wrong with you?' He didn't seem to know or care what he said.

'Be careful, you're saying too much,' she warned, but he did not hear her.

'I'll bring you up to date. I'll soon bring you up to date. Two nights ago I went to a hotel in the Black Forest. The Germans aren't stuck in the dark ages. We were ten couples. A divorced woman was with me. Helga. Every man had two keys to his room. After drinks, each man threw a key on the table and went to his room. The women stayed behind to pick up a key. The woman who came to my room said when she opened the door, 'I won the prize. I got the Irishman.' We did everything man or beast can do and we were the last couple to come down. Everybody clapped as soon as we came into the bar and wanted to buy us drinks. You mightn't think much of these people, but they know what I am worth.'

'This time you've gone too far,' she said.

'Not half far enough.' He came towards her. 'You'll either do what you're supposed to do in this house or get out.' He seized her with both hands and raced her to the door. She tried to stop herself falling as she was flung but before she realized what had happened she found herself reeling to a stop in the middle of the small lawn. She didn't fall. Behind her she heard the door lock.

It was cold and later than she thought. She was wearing a cardigan over a light dress. Not a single television set flickered behind the curtains of the little road. No music played anywhere. She thought of the children. She knew they would be safe and she could not go back to the house again. A car went slowly past on the main road. She would walk. She went out from the bungalows into the centre of town. A man was standing at one of the corners and shifted his feet and coughed as she passed. A full moon above the roofs shone down.

She started to sob, then to laugh headily before she regained a sort of calm. Once she left the street lamps of the town, the moon gave her a long shadow for company. Now and then she broke into short runs. The cold never quite left her shoulders.

So intent was she on getting to her mother's house that it closed out all other thoughts. Close to the lake she smelt the rank waterweed and the sharp wild mint. The moon was amazing on the lake, flooding the water in yellow light, making it appear as deep as the sky. The path through the fields was sharp and clear above the lake. Around the house it was like day. She tapped on the bedroom window, but Maggie was already awake.

As she told her mother what happened, Kate was suddenly so

tired that listening to her own voice was like listening to the voice of another. Even with the children there, awake or sleeping, the bungalow that had been locked against her seemed as far away as Africa.

As Michael Doherty hadn't a car at that time, Maggie cycled round the lake to ask if I'd drive them into town the next morning. There was trouble and Kate needed to see the solicitor. They were waiting at the lake gate an hour later. Kate looked pale but beautiful that morning. She was unusual in that she grew more beautiful with age. Maggie's face was always interesting but never beautiful. Except for paleness and tiredness nobody could have guessed from either of them that anything was wrong.

We stopped at the mart on the way into town. The great spaces were empty. A few beasts waiting within the sheds were lowing and listening before lowing again. Compared to the bellowing of market days, the lowing of the isolated animals sounded hollow and lonely and futile. When Kate came from the mart she told us that she had telephoned the school. Their father had taken the children to school that morning. From the mart Maggie and Kate went together to the solicitor's.

Old Mr Gannon received them. He was now partly retired but had been very fond of Kate ever since she'd worked for him as a young woman, but the advice he had to give them wasn't good. By leaving the matrimonial home, Kate had forfeited all her rights. She couldn't, though, be stopped from entering their house to see the children. Neither could her husband prevent her from leaving the house.

Kate went to work in the mart, and I drove Maggie home. She told me everything on the way. 'I know you won't talk.' Kate was going straight from work to see the children. I said I'd drive them anywhere they wanted to be driven to over the next few days. That is how I came to take Kate and her belongings from the house late that same night.

Maggie asked me to stay in the car while she went into the bungalow. Kate opened the door and it was kept open. I saw the children near the door and once I thought I saw Harkin's shadow fall across the light. The two women started carrying loose clothes and a suitcase out of the house. It was a relief to get out of the car to open the boot and the back doors, besides sitting and watching in the mirrors. I only got back into the car when I saw the women kissing the children. The boy was clinging to them, but the two girls looked withdrawn.

It wasn't anything you'd want to watch too often. Kate cried in the back all the way out, but at the lake she was the first out to open that gate. She told us not to wait while she closed the gate. She wanted to walk the rest of the way in. Maggie and I had all her belongings taken from the car by the time she crossed the yard. She had stopped crying.

'I'm sorry,' she said to me as she came in.

'There's nothing to be sorry about.'

'I should have more control,' she said as she reached into the press for the whiskey bottle and poured me a large glass. Neither Kate nor Maggie ever drank. I dislike drinking on my own, but it was easier to drink than to refuse. I drank the whiskey down and left. I could see that the two women were tired out of their minds.

I drove Kate in and out of town for most of a week. Maggie always came with me when I went to the house at night. I never saw Harkin once on any of these nights. They were worried about taking up too much of my time and tried to give me money. I would gladly have driven Kate in and out for a whole year, but when she found rooms above the hairdressing salon on Main Street I wasn't needed any more. The one thing I wasn't sorry to miss was seeing the way Kate looked as we drove away from the house each night.

A slow, hard battle began, all of it silent and underground. Nothing ever came out into the open. After work she went to the house and stayed with the children till their bedtime. Harkin never spoke. As he would not allow her to cook or eat in the house, she delayed coming until after they'd eaten. Weekends were the worst. Often she would turn up at the house and find it locked. He would have taken the children with him on his rounds of the houses.

Once when she suggested that she take the children out to Maggie's for the weekend, he stared at her in silence before turning away. Gradually the children got used to their changed lives. There were times when they complained that she was not like other mothers. Knowing this, she was careful in everything she did outside the house. After more than a year had gone by, on certain evenings she found an attractive German woman in the house. On those evenings she left early.

When Jerome Callaghan was in the mart on business, he would nearly always come into the office. His ease and charm only increased her wariness. The silence between herself and Harkin over the children was like inching across a glass roof. She could risk nothing. She could only live within the small worlds of her work at the mart, her mother's house and company, the haven of her own rooms and the cramped confines she was allowed with her children. If Kate had continued living with her husband, any sexual attraction she held for Jerome Callaghan would have been suppressed, but once she left the house and moved into rooms, that changed. He was not put off that she gave no sign of reciprocating his interest. It was in his nature to be patient and he was used to getting his way.

At school Jerome Callaghan had belonged with Kate to a small group distinctly better than the rest, and he belonged there easily, without effort. He could have gone to university, but instead went to work in his uncle's insurance and auctioneering business in the town. Again, without much effort, he succeeded in expanding the business while getting on well with his uncle, his mother's brother, who had never married, and when the uncle retired it was Callaghan who took over.

Once the business was his own, he left it as it was. Hardly anything changed. The uncle came in to work as before, and often they had lunch together at the Royal Hotel. His nature was so well known that he was never suspected of courting the uncle in the hope of inheriting his money; and when his uncle died leaving him everything, the plain grief he showed did not look put on like a dark suit for the day.

His uncle had been an original shareholder in the mart, and when Callaghan asked Kate to see McNulty, he was using the manager as a cover. The position was already Kate's for the taking. While his modest way of life and manner and the underplaying of his increasing wealth were greatly approved of, his sexual inclination was nowhere liked. From a very young age he was drawn to older women: 'Callaghan doesn't want the trouble of schooling them; he likes his breaching done,' was joked to cover suspicion and resentment of any deviation.

An affair with the headmistress of the school Kate's children attended continued over several years, an intelligent, dark gypsy of a woman who had many suitors once but had let the years run on without naming a wedding day. No matter how much care or discretion was used, word of this and other affairs always got out. On a Friday evening the headmistress would leave her car at the railway station. Callaghan would meet her at a distant station, and they would drive away towards two whole nights and days together; but there was nearly always someone connected with the town who saw them in a hotel or restaurant or bar, and once, during the long school holiday, together on a London street. Harkin and Callaghan viewed one another with innate dislike. Callaghan was working for his uncle when Harkin first came to town. Football didn't interest him, and he resented the popular athlete's easy assumption of an animal superiority. Spoiled with adulation, Harkin saw the polite but firm distance Callaghan kept as criticism, all the more chafing since it was too hidden to be challenged.

Once Harkin became involved with the tourists, an involvement that led naturally to property dealing, he was probably relieved to be able to turn their mutual antipathy into rivalry because of the enormous change in the strength of their relative positions over the years. All property dealings that came his way he directed towards Callaghan's competitors, and now he was moving to set up as an auctioneer in his own right.

'What does Callaghan ever do but fiddle with old ladies' buttons while lying in wait for any easy game that comes along?'

A change had come to Callaghan's life that made him more vulnerable than he knew. His beloved mother died. His brother married. The newly married couple's protestations when he suggested that he should move and leave them to their own young lives—'You're no trouble to us at all, only help, and we hardly ever see you anyhow'—strengthened his conviction that he should move out into his own life; but what life? Lazily he had believed that one day he'd marry a young woman, a doctor or a teacher, somebody with work and interests of her own. Years before, he'd bought part of an estate by a lake, with mature woods, oak and beech and larch. Above the lake he'd built a house he neither finished nor furnished, never making up his mind whether it was to be his life or an investment he would sell on a rising market. Several times he thought of finishing the house and going to live there while continuing to live with his brother and sister-in-law. During all this time he was careful not to pester Kate, and, if anything, visited her office in the mart less often than before, but the small courtesies he showed her could not be mistaken. When he did ask her openly out for an evening, she was able both to meet and turn aside the open sexual nature of the invitation.

'We're old school friends. We know one another too well,' she said.

'That's not knowing,' he smiled but did not press her further.

He appeared no longer to be seeing any of the women he had been linked with. Most weekends he spent alone about the town, unheard of before, weekends when she, as often as not, found the bungalow empty and locked, and they could not avoid running into one another.

'I'm not free,' she said to him bluntly when they had coffee together in the hotel one Saturday. She had come back into the town after finding the house deserted, the car gone.

'How not free? You live alone.'

'I don't even feel safe to be seen with you here over coffee in daylight.'

'Why?'

'Talk. Rumour. You know how little it needs to be fed.'

'Such scruples do not seem to bother your husband.'

'That's his business,' she told him sharply. 'He has charge of the children.'

'You are worried about losing the children?'

'I think of nothing else.'

She asked him as a favour to stay behind when she left. She wanted to be seen leaving alone. He agreed readily, ordered fresh coffee and was soon joined by two men from the bar who wanted to discuss a property deal.

One of the few liberties she was allowed with the children was to take them to Mass. One Sunday came when she found the children gone and the house locked. Always the same excuse was used—when any excuse was offered—that the children were taken with him on his rounds of the tourist houses for their own safety. She became very upset and decided to walk all the way to the lake to talk to Maggie before going back to the solicitor to see if there was any way she could obtain more regular fixed access. Every week there was some new twist or difficulty. She was afraid that soon she would not get to see her children at all, Jim and Kate and young Maggie, all brought up in the same air and world, and all so different. As she walked outside the town with these images and anxieties moving through her mind, sometimes with the charm of their individual faces and endearing gestures before her, and then again turning away from her with the woodiness of placards or a picket line, a car drew in ahead of her. Before she recognized the car or driver she knew it was Jerome Callaghan.

'I was just passing,' he said when he saw her reluctance to enter the car.

'I don't want to avoid you but I can't afford to be seen with you either.'

'I'm offering a lift. That's all,' he said.

'It's too dangerous.' He saw she was not herself, excited and troubled.

'I'm just going that way,' he said.

'An hour ago I called to the house and it was shut; the children gone again. I'm not free. Sometimes I think I'm worse off now than before I got the job in the mart.'

'You are free as far as I'm concerned.'

'I'm aware of that.' She smiled. 'I'm still not free as far as I'm concerned.'

'And I'm ready to help you in any way I can—and even wait.'

At the lake gate he stopped the car, and as she was about to shut the door, she said, 'If you'd like to come in to meet my mother, you are welcome.'

'Maggie and I have known each other for years.'

'We'll have to drive, then. The car would be seen by too many at the gate.'

John McGahern

When the car crossed the hill and was going down to the house under the tall trees, he eased it to a stop, letting the engine run.

'What's going to happen to us?' he asked.

'I don't see how someone like you would want to get involved in my situation.'

'I love you.'

In spite of his rational or common-sense self, he'd been drawn into the town in the early morning because of nothing but her presence in the rooms above the hairdresser's. He had this obsessional desire to see her, if only with her children at Mass. He'd watched her leave the rooms and walk to the bungalow on the outskirts of the town. From a safe distance he'd observed her attempts to enter the locked house. When he saw her walk out of the town in the direction of the lake, he guessed where she was going.

'You are only making things bad for yourself. Even if I wanted to help, there is nothing I can do. You see how I am. It is as if I've already had my life.'

'What's going to happen?'

'I don't know but I know it can't go on like this. On Achill it was this bad, but in a different way, and I knew then it couldn't go on. I knew something had to happen. What happened was the last thing I wanted or wished, but it did happen. I have the same feeling that something is about to happen now that will change everything. It has to happen.'

'Tell me one thing. It is all I ask. If you were free, would you be interested at all?'

'Yes. But what use is that?'

'It's use to me. I know you well enough to know you would not say it for the sake of saying. Even I feel something has to happen. I hope to God it can set us free.'

She thought of kissing him lightly but then drew back. She had not even that right. He drove to the house. In the house he had tea with the two women and chatted agreeably with Maggie before leaving them alone after a half-hour.

If they had kissed when the car was stopped under the trees that went down to the house, if they had even lain bone to bone in the empty night above Main Street in the solace and healing that flesh can bring to hurt desire, they would not have gone halfway to satisfy all the rife rumour implied they did with one another: 'Old Ireland is coming along at a great rate. There was a time you lay on the bed you made, but now it's all just the same as a change of oil or tyres. The Harkins have split. Harkin has a German woman and scores of others when he feels like rising. The heart, my dear, may be wobbly but it appears everything is healthy enough in other departments. The wife, I hear, hasn't let any grass grow either. She works at the mart and is seen with Jerome Callaghan, who, they say, can tip a cat on the way out through a skylight. Yes, my dear, old Ireland is certainly coming along.' None of those who discoursed so freely above supermarket trolleys or bar counters, or just standing or sitting about, could trace their words to any source, but it did not lessen the authority with which they spoke. I even heard things quoted that I was supposed to have said of which I had never spoken a word.

At the height of these rumours, Harkin came all the way round the lake to see me. I was in the house when I heard the beat of a heavy diesel. I listened for it to go past the gate, but the sound stopped. After a while, a low tapping came on the front door. A small boy stood outside. I failed to recognize him.

'Daddy wants to see you.'

'Who's Daddy?'

'Guard Harkin.'

'What does he want?' It was too late now to try to make any amends to the boy. If he had been with Kate or Maggie, I'd have known him and given him coins or chocolate or cake or apples.

'He said he wants to see you.'

Harkin sat beside the wheel of the blue Mercedes outside the gate in the shade of the alders. His door was thrown open. The two girls sat in the back. He had put on a great deal of weight since his playing days. His features had coarsened. I assumed he did not get out of the car because of his heart condition.

'What kind of fish are in the lake?' he demanded though he already knew. He had helped to net the lake.

'Pike, eel, perch . . . '

'Is there much?'

'Not any more. They say the tourists netted the lake.'

'The foreigners are blamed for everything nowadays.'

'I wouldn't know.'

'Of course you wouldn't know but you'd talk.'

'The boy said you wanted to see me. Is there something you want?'

'I just wanted to get a look at you,' he said and shut the car door. I watched him back the Mercedes away from the gate and turn down to the lake, the children grave and silent in the back.

Maggie told me Jerome Callaghan came alone a few times to the house during those months. She also said there was never truth in the rumours flying around about him and Kate. He liked Kate and wished to help her, but that was all there ever was to it. Maggie was right and wasn't right.

One evening Kate left the children early because the German woman was making her presence felt in the house. She was walking back towards Main Street when Callaghan's car drew up. He wanted to take her to see his unfinished house.

'It's too dark for us to be seen, and it's normal for the car to be driving there.'

The night was dark. She had to imagine the woods on either side, the lake in darkness below the house, the mountains at the back. When the front light came on, she saw a small concrete mixer, a barrow and wooden planks scattered about on what could have been intended as a long lawn. A paint-splattered table stood in the centre of the large living room with some wooden chairs. All the other rooms were empty and held hollow echoes.

'It came cheap on the market, another man's misfortune, but I've never been able to let it go. I know they laugh: "Callaghan's built a big cage without first finding a bird."'

Kate went with him from room to room, looking with curiosity at everything but without speaking. As they prepared to leave, she said, 'It could be a fine house. A rich man's house.'

'Maybe some day,' he said, and she was glad he did not complete the wish. Without touching or speaking, they had drawn very close, as if they were two single people setting out on a journey from which they could return together. On the outskirts of the town

she asked him to stop the car so that she could walk in to the first
street light alone but before she left the car she kissed him firmly
on the lips. 'I know it's dangerous and I can promise nothing.'

The silent, almost unbearable strain in the evenings with Harkin
and the children changed without warning. He became
alarmingly friendly. He must have heard some rumour about
Callaghan and Kate. The German woman disappeared from the
house. His voice could not have been more conciliatory when he
spoke to her for the first time in months.

'We want to forget everything, Kate. We'll start all over
again, as if nothing happened.'

She could find no words. She was grateful for the noise of a
passing car. 'It's too sudden,' she said. 'I don't know what to say.'

'We want you to think about it anyhow. The children want
that as well.' Later he asked, 'Have you thought about it, Kate?'

'For the children I'd do anything, but I don't see how we . . .'
Mercifully she was able to leave the rest unsaid.

'Will you think about it? We all want to get back to square
one. All the children as much as myself.'

Harkin and the children were there every time she called that
week. The friendliness increased. Her nervousness grew intense.
She had to force herself to go to the house.

'Will you be coming back to the house at the end of the
week, Mammy?' young Kate asked as they were playing draughts
together before their bedtime. She'd been playing badly, and the
girls were beating her easily.

'I don't think so, love.'

'Daddy said we'd all be happy again,' little Kate added.

'I know,' she said.

She told Jerome Callaghan about the new pressure she had
come under to return to the marriage, the way the whole weather
of the house had turned.

'What will you do?'

'I can't go back. I know everything is about to change. That
is all I know.'

'Do you think you should go to the house at all?'

'I have no choice. I have no other way to see the children.'

The next day Maggie came into town, and they spent a long time talking. They agreed to go together the following week to see a young solicitor Jerome Callaghan had recommended, no matter what happened. When Kate went to see the children that evening, it was Callaghan who drove Maggie out to the lake. Kate was sick at work the next day but couldn't be persuaded to go home. In the evening Jerome Callaghan insisted on driving her to her rooms, and she allowed him to come with her into the house in full view of the busy evening street. She seemed to be past caring; but when he offered to drive her to the bungalow after they had tea together she responded fiercely. 'You must be out of your mind.'

'In that case, I'm waiting here, and if you're not back before eleven I'm coming to look for you.'

'I'll be back before eleven,' she said.

As soon as she entered the house, she saw the strain in Harkin's friendliness.

'Well, have you made up your mind?'

She was calmer now. She said it was impossible. She felt the stone-faced silence return. Only by shutting everything out and going from moment to small moment with the children was she able to get through the long evening which suddenly started to race as the time to leave drew near.

The two girls were reserved as she kissed them goodnight. She was afraid the boy would cling to her so she lifted him high in the air. Beforehand she had been eating currants nervously from a glass jar on the sideboard and she lifted him awkwardly because the currants were still in her hand and she did not want them to scatter.

'I want you to know that if you leave tonight you'll never set foot in this house again.'

She bowed her head. 'I'll have to take that risk.' As she turned her back she heard a sharp click but did not turn to see him lift the gun. One hand was reaching for the door when she fell, the other closed tight. When it was opened, it held a fistful of small black currants.

Jerome Callaghan sat waiting without moving in the one chair. Not until after ten did he begin to grow anxious. At half past ten he moved to the window. Several times he went to leave, then held back, but once the hand of his watch moved past eleven, he ran down the stairs and drove to Harkin's house. A Garda car already blocked the entrance to the short road. There were other police cars in the street. The guard and Callaghan knew one another well.

'There's been a shooting. Mrs Harkin . . . '

'Is she . . . ?'

'I'm sorry,' Guard Sullivan said.

Callaghan restrained the urge to rush to her, the futile wish to help and succour what can be helped no longer, and turned slowly back to his car. Numbly he turned the car around and found himself driving out to the lake, parking at the gate. As he got out, he disturbed wildfowl in the reeds along the shore, and they scattered, shrieking, towards the centre. There was no moon but there were clear reflections on the water. Never did life seem so mysterious and inhospitable. They might as well all be out there in the middle of the lake with the wildfowl.

The lights were on in the house. When he knocked, Maggie came to the door. Later when the guards called at the house with word of the death, it was Callaghan who answered the knock.

After being charged, Harkin was transferred to a mental institution for a psychiatric report as part of the preparations for his trial. He took great interest in his case and consulted regularly with his solicitor. He tried but was unable to prevent the children from going to Maggie. Other than his solicitor, the only person he asked to see was Guard McCarthy, who had fought back to back with him against the tinkers on that terrible night years before.

McCarthy had settled in Cork and married a teacher. When Harkin's letter arrived, he was alarmed and took it straight to his sergeant, who consulted his superiors. To McCarthy's dismay, he was asked to visit his old friend and to write down everything that was said during the visit in case it could be of use in the forthcoming trial. All the expenses of the visit would be paid by the state.

On a summer's day the two men met and were allowed through locked doors into a walled ornamental garden. They sat on a wooden bench by a small fountain. Almost playfully Harkin examined McCarthy's ear for stitchmarks and asked, 'Do you think Cork has much of a chance in the All-Ireland this year?'

'Not much,' McCarthy answered. A silence followed that seemed to take a great age. The visit could not end quickly enough for him.

'What makes you say that?' Harkin eventually asked.

'The team is uneven. They're short of at least two forwards.'

'I'd hate to see Dublin winning it again.'

'They have the population,' McCarthy said. 'They have the pick.'

There was another long silence until Harkin asked, 'How do you think my case will go?'

In the heart-stopping pause that followed, McCarthy could hear the water splashing from the fountain, the birds singing. He said he had no earthly clue. The silence returned, but nothing came to break it. 'Was there anything in particular you wanted to see me about, Michael?' he ventured cautiously.

'No. Nothing. I just wanted to get a look at you again after all these years,' and he placed his hand on the guard's shoulder as they both rose.

McCarthy wrote down everything that Harkin said, but it was never used as evidence. That same evening Harkin swallowed an array of tablets that he had managed to conceal, and before he slipped into unconsciousness he reached beneath the scar on his chest to tear out the mechanism that regulated his heartbeat.

A silence came down around all that happened. Nobody complained about the normal quiet. Bird cries were sweet. The wing-beat of the swan crossing the house gave strength. The long light of day crossing the lake steeped us in privilege and mystery and infinite reflections that nobody wanted to break or question.

Gradually the sense of quiet weakened. The fact that nothing much was happening ceased to comfort. A craving for change began again. The silence around the murder was broken. All sorts of blame was apportioned as we noticed each year that passed across the face of the lake, quickening and gathering speed before swinging round again, until crowds of years seemed suddenly in the air above the lake, all gathering for flight.

With the years, Maggie and I had drawn closer. Whenever I had to go into the town I nearly always called at her house to see if she wanted to come and I often took the children to the train or met them when they came for weekends from Dublin.

All three children were at university. They were well mannered and intelligent and anxious to please, but compared to Maggie's rootedness they were like shadows. It was as if none of them could quite believe they had full rights to be alive on earth under the sky like every single other.

Every year I drove Maggie to the Christmas dinner and party for senior citizens in the parish hall. I am now almost old enough to go to the dinner in my own right, but it is one meal I want to put off for as long as I can. When Maggie was made Senior Citizen of the Year, it was natural that I'd drive her to Carrick for the presentation. All of us who knew her were delighted, but there was great difficulty in getting her to accept.

'Well, all of us here think it's great, Maggie, no matter what you say,' I said to her as we drove to Carrick.

'It's a lot of bother,' she answered. 'The old people used always to say it was never lucky to be too noticed. The shady corners are safer.'

'Even the shady corners may be safe no longer, but isn't it wonderful how well all the children did, and all you were able to do for them.'

'They were no trouble. They did it all themselves. I think they were making sure they'd never be left behind a second time,' and then she laughed her old, deep laugh. 'The two lassies will be fine, but I'm not so sure if his lordship will last the course. When he set out to be a doctor I don't think he realized he was in for seven years. Now his head is full of nothing but girls and discos. He thinks I'm made of money.'

As Maggie entered the ballroom of the hotel, everybody stood, and there was spontaneous clapping as she was led to her place. I saw Jerome Callaghan and his young wife at one of the tables. It was said he gave Maggie all the help she would allow over the years in bringing up the children—and I can't imagine her ever taking very much—and that he had played a part in her being chosen. I waited until she was seated behind an enormous vase of roses. Then I left as we had agreed. I walked about the empty town, had one drink in a quiet bar that also sold shoes and boots, across from the town clock, until it was time to take Maggie home.

'How did you enjoy it anyhow?' I asked as we drove towards the lake.

'Enjoy it?' she laughed. 'I suppose they meant well but I wouldn't like to go through the likes of tonight too often. The whole lot of them would lighten your head. What did I do? I did nothing. What else could I do? I was—in life.'

She was silent then until we turned in round the lake. 'Even where I am now, it's still all very interesting. Sometimes even far, far too interesting.'

The moon was bright on the lake, turning it into a clear, still sky. The fields above the lake and the dark shapes of the hedges stood out. Maggie sat quietly in the car while I got out to open the gate. Only a few short years before she would have insisted on getting out and walking the whole way in on her own. Wildfowl scattered from the reeds along the shore out towards the centre of the lake as soon as the car door opened. They squawked and shrieked for a while before turning into a dark silent huddle. Close by, a white moon rested on the water. There was no wind. The stars in their places were clear and fixed. Who would want change since change will come without wanting? Who this night would not want to live? □

HAROLD PINTER
A NOTE ON SHAKESPEARE

I wrote 'A Note' in 1951, when I was touring with Anew MacMaster, the Shakespearean actor-manager, throughout Southern Ireland. We presented a different play every night (seven nights a week and two matinées) and our repertoire included *Hamlet, The Merchant of Venice, Julius Caesar, As You Like it, Macbeth, King Lear* and *Othello.*

Mac generally took two nights off a week when the rest of the company performed plays like *The Importance of Being Earnest, An Ideal Husband, Rope* and *An Inspector Calls* but Shakespeare dominated our lives. I had in any case been obsessed with him in the preceding four years but to find myself actually performing in his plays with the extraordinary Anew MacMaster was an electric experience. Anyway, this 'Note' came out of an active and living engagement with the work in hand both on the page and in the theatre.

The mistake they make, most of them, is to attempt to determine and calculate, with the finest instruments, the source of the wound.

They seek out the gaps between the apparent and the void that hinges upon it with all due tautness. They turn to the wound with deference, a lance, and a needle and thread.

At the entrance of the lance the gap widens. At the use of needle and thread the wound coagulates and atrophies in their hands.

Shakespeare writes of the open wound and, through him, we know it open and know it closed. We tell when it ceases to beat and tell it at its highest peak of fever.

In attempting to approach Shakespeare's work in its entirety, you are called upon to grapple with a perspective in which the horizon alternately collapses and reforms behind you, in which the mind's participation is subject to an intense diversity of atmospheric.

Once the investigation has begun, however, there is no other way but to him.

One discovers a long corridor of postures; fluid and hardened at the quick; gross and godlike; putrescent and copulative; raddled; attentive; crippled and gargantuan; crumbling with the dropsy; heavy with elephantiasis; broody with government; severe; fanatical; paralytic; voluptuous; impassive; muscle-bound; lissom; virginal; unwashed; bewildered; humpbacked; icy and statuesque. All are contained in the wound which Shakespeare does not attempt to sew up or reshape, whose pain he does not attempt to eradicate. He amputates, deadens, aggravates at will, within the limits of a particular piece, but he will not pronounce judgement or cure. Such comment as there is is so variously split up between characters and so contradictory in itself that no central point of opinion or inclining can be determined.

He himself is trapped in his own particular order, and is unable to go out at a distance to regulate and forestall abortion or lapses in *vraisemblance*. He can only rely on a 'few well-chosen words' to bring him through any doubtful patch.

He belongs of course, ultimately, to a secret society, a conspiracy, of which there is only one member: himself. In that sense, and in a number of others too, he is a malefactor; a lunatic; a deserter; a conscientious objector; a guttersnipe; a social menace and an Antichrist.

He is also a beggar; a road sweeper; a tinker; a hashish-drinker; a leper; a chicken-fancier; a paper-seller; a male nurse; a sun-worshipper and a gibbering idiot.

He is no less a traffic policeman; a rowing blue; a rear gunner; a chartered accountant; a best man; a bus-conductor; a paid guide; a marriage guidance counsellor; a churchgoer; a stage carpenter; an umpire; an acrobat and a Clerk of the Court.

His tongue is guttural, Arabic, pepperish, composed, parsimonious, voluminous, rabid, diarrhoetic, transparent, laundered, dainty, mellifluous, consonantal, stammering, scabrous, naked, blade-edged, one-legged, piercing, hushed, clinical, dumb, convulsed, lewd, vicious, voracious, inane, Tibetan, monosyllabic, epileptic, raucous, ministerial, sudden, Sudanese, palpitating, thunderous, earthy, whimsical, acrimonious, wintry, malicious, fearsome, blighted, blistered, mouldy, tantalizing, juicy, innocent, lordly, gluttonous, irreverent, blasphemous, avaricious, autumnal, blasted, ecstatic, necromantic, gentle, venomous, somnambulistic, monotonous, uproarious, feverish, austere, demented, deathly, fractious, obsessed, ironic, palsied, morbid, sanctimonious, sacrilegious, calm, cunning, cannibalistic and authoritative.

He moves through all with a vehement and flexible control. He turns and bites his own tail. He defecates on his own carpet. He repeats the Bible sideways. He disdains the communication cord and the lifebelt. He scratches his head with an iceberg. But the fabric never breaks. The tightrope is never at less than an even stretch. He aborts, he meanders, he loses his track, he overshoots his mark, he drops his glasses, he meets himself coming back, he digresses, he calumniates, he alters direction, he sinks in at the knees, he rolls over like a log, he forgets the drift, he drops someone flat, he exaggerates, oversimplifies, disrupts, falsifies, evades the issue, is carried home drunk; he dawdles, he dwindles, he trips over his own feet, he runs away with himself, he implicates others, he misses the point, he ends up at the same place, he falls back on geometry, he cheats, he squanders, he leaves it at that; he gets in his own way, he burns his fingers, he turns turtle, he stews in his own juice, he loses all hands; suffers fire, arsony, rape, loot, ravage, fraud, bondage, murder, interference, snobbery, lice, jealousy, snakebites, damp beds, falling arches, jugglery, quackery, mastoids, bunions, hailstones, bladder trouble, fainting fits, eye strain, morning sickness, heat, dirt, riot, plague, suicide. He suffers, commits and survives them all.

The fabric never breaks. The wound is open. The wound is peopled. ☐

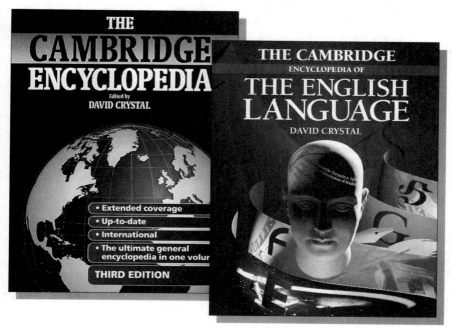

NOTES ON CONTRIBUTORS

RENE BELLETTO was born in 1945. He is a scriptwriter, guitar teacher, poet and novelist. His novel *L'Enfer* won the Prix Fémina.

BRIAN CATHCART is a freelance writer, formerly foreign editor and deputy editor of the *Independent on Sunday*. He lives in London.

PATRICK CHAMOISEAU lives in Martinique. His novel *Texaco* won the Prix Goncourt in 1992. 'The Rat' is taken from his memoir, *Childhood* (Gallimard, Paris, 1994). Carol Volk's translation will be published by the University of Nebraska Press in 1998.

JOHN DAVIES is a landscape photographer whose work has been exhibited at the Victoria and Albert Museum in London, and the Museum of Modern Art in New York. He lives in Cardiff.

RAYMOND DEPARDON is a Magnum photographer and documentary film-maker. His photographic record of the farm near Villefranche where he was born in 1942, *La Ferme du Garet*, was published in 1995 (Editions Carré).

ASSIA DJEBAR was born in Algeria. She was the first Algerian woman to attend the Ecole normale supérieure in Sèvres, and the first to become a professor of history in North Africa. 'A Sentence of Love' is taken from the collection of short stories *Oran, Langue morte* (Actes Sud).

MICHEL HOUELLEBECQ is a novelist and poet who cites as influences Neil Young, Schubert and Nietzsche. 'We Are the Kings' is taken from *L'Extension du Domaine de la Lutte*, Paul Hammond's translation of which will be published by Serpent's Tail in 1998. He lives in Paris.

IVAN KLÍMA's novels include *My Golden Trades, Love and Garbage* and *Judge on Trial*. 'Don't Forsake Me' is taken from *The Ultimate Intimacy*, which will be published by Granta Books in November 1997.

CAROLINE LAMARCHE lives near Brussels. Her second novel, *Le Jour du Chien* (Minuit) won the Prix Rossel. 'Night in the Afternoon' is taken from her first novel, *La Nuit l'Après-Midi*, and is the first English translation of her work.

DAVID MACEY is working on a biography of Frantz Fanon, which will be published by Granta Books in 1998. He has published a biography of Michel Foucault. He lives in Leeds.

JOHN MCGAHERN lives in County Leitrim, Ireland. His novels include *The Leavetaking, The Pornographer* and *Amongst Women*, which was shortlisted for the 1990 Booker Prize.

PIERRE MERLE is a Paris-based journalist. His dictionary of modern slang, *Le Dico de l'Argot fin de siècle*, was published by Seuil in 1997.

HAROLD PINTER's play *Moonlight*, directed by Karel Reisz, opens on 25 September at the Théâtre Rond Point, Paris. *Ashes to Ashes* opens in Palermo, Sicily, in October.

LUC SANTE was born in Verviers, Belgium and now lives in New York. 'Lingua Franca' is taken from *The Factory of Facts*, which will be published by Granta Books in 1998.